RICHARD ARTSCHWAGER
PUBLIC (public)

September 14–November 10, 1991

Organized by Russell Panczenko

With essays by Germano Celant,
Herbert Muschamp, and Russell Panczenko

Elvehjem Museum of Art
University of Wisconsin–Madison

ILLUSTRATION ACKNOWLEDGMENTS

Photograph on page 18 Eric Baum; photgraphs on pages 19, 21, 22, 26, 27, 28, 31, 32, 33, 34, 56 (fig. 9), 59, 61, 62, 65, 66, 70, (5), 72 (9) copyright © Dorothy Zeidman; photographs on pages 24 and 71 (7) copyright © Douglas M. Parker

ISBN 0–932900–28–3

Library of Congress Catalog Card Number 91–75567

CONTENTS

FOREWORD

On September 14, 1991, the Elvehjem Museum of Art inaugurated *Generations*, a newly completed outdoor sculpture by Richard Artschwager. *Generations*, whose granite and steel components spread across the grounds in front of the building converting the area into a public plaza, is radically site specific, straining to an extreme the conceptual boundaries that exist between sculpture, architecture, and landscaping. In addition, the Elvehjem sculpture includes several untraditional elements such as lights and trees situated twenty-two feet in the air. In order to give the commissioned work, which is permanently located in front of the Elvehjem, an art historical and critical context as well as to introduce it to the Madison community, the museum organized the exhibition *Richard Artschwager: PUBLIC (public)*. The exhibition is intended as an educational vehicle which will promote discussion, understanding, and acceptance of the new sculpture as well as inspire further interest in public art and its related issues.

The exhibition is articulated into two distinct parts, the first, curated by the artist himself, includes nineteen paintings and sculptures borrowed from a variety of collectors around the United States. Although this group of objects, dating from 1962 to the present, represents a comprehensive look at Artschwager's career, it is not intended as a reflection in miniature of the retrospective exhibition of the artist's work organized by the Whitney Museum of American Art in 1988. Instead, the Elvehjem, based on its experience of having artists present slide lectures about their own work, invited the Artschwager to select a group of works which, in his opinion, reflected his long and productive career. Such an approach provided the artist with the opportunity to make a personal statement about his own development, an opportunity which had never before been afforded him. The second part of the exhibition focuses on Artschwager's twelve outdoor projects and comprises models from the artist's personal collection and photographic enlargements of the completed pieces in situ. This group of works, which remains relatively unknown, begins with *Transactions* of 1982, his first exploration into outdoor works, and culminates in *Generations*, his most recent commission. Seven of these works, beginning with the untitled bicycle rack, constructed in Münster, Germany in 1987, have been realized; the others exist only in model form.

The present catalogue follows the double structure of the exhibition. It begins with a new critical overview of Artschwager's work by Germano Celant, curator of contemporary art at the Solomon R. Gug-

genheim Museum, which incorporates the works selected by the artist for the Elvehjem exhibition. The second part is subdivided into two sections. The first, prepared by the present author, includes a documentation of the Elvehjem's selection process, which awarded the commission to Richard Artschwager, and the creation of *Generations*. In addition, it includes an illustrated checklist of Artschwager's twelve outdoor projects, completed pieces being reproduced in color, models in black and white. The final essay was prepared by Herbert Muschamp, head of the department of architectural criticism at the Parsons School of Design, who explores the relation between Artschwager's outdoor works and architecture.

In addition to acknowledging the scholarly contributions of the two guest authors, on behalf of myself and the Elvehjem, I wish to thank particularly Tom MacGregor, Richard Artschwager's professional colleague and business manager. Mr. MacGregor provided not only essential information and extensive assistance with all aspects of this project but also his personal enthusiasm and insights into the work and creative process of the artist, which were informative, inspiring, and invaluable. Without Mr. MacGregor's generous cooperation *PUBLIC (public)* would not have been possible.

Several individuals and institutions graciously lent their works to the present exhibition. In this regard, the Elvehjem owes a special debt of gratitude to the following.

Primary funding for *PUBLIC (public)* was generously provided by the Norman Bassett Foundation, the Lannan Foundation, and the National Endowment for the Arts, a federal agency. Additional funding for the exhibition was made available by the Wisconsin Arts Board and the Dane County Cultural Affairs Commission.

The creation of *Generations* itself was made possible by a special grant by the Anonymous Fund Committee, a University of Wisconsin–Madison Trust Fund, John H. Van Vleck General Art Purchase Fund, Cyril W. Nave Endowment Fund, and Elvehjem Museum of Art General Endowment Fund. The initial kindness and enthusiasm of Judy and Howard D. Hirsch opened the door to the whole enterprise by permitting the Elvehjem to gather five consultants in Madison and begin the search for an artist for the Elvehjem commission.

The museum especially wants to acknowledge, for their commitment and aesthetic acumen, the Elvehjem's sculpture committee: Dean Don Crawford; Professors Barbara Buenger, Frank Horlbeck, Patricia

Mansfield, and Wayne Taylor; Horst Lobe, senior architect of the university's Department of Planning and Construction; and the indefatigable Elvehjem Council member, Jane Coleman.

I would also like to extend here special gratitude to the emeritus Dean of the College of Letters and Science, E. David Cronon, whose unwavering support of the Elvehjem and commitment to the sculpture project provided the impetus to realize the new outdoor sculpture.

The museum also appreciates the time and efforts on behalf of the new sculpture spent by various contractors and university employees, especially the staff members of the university's Physical Plant.

It is all too often forgotten that museum directors rely on a competent staff to handle the numerous details of installing an exhibition and producing a catalogue. Elvehjem staff members whose work was indispensable to the present project are editor Patricia Powell for editing the catalogue, registrar Lindy Waites and assistant registrar Sandy Rogers for managing shipping and photographing of works, assistant director for administration Corinne Magnoni for coordinating practical and financial matters, Lori DeMeuse for keeping accounts in good order, and preparators Dale Malner and William Gilmore for installing the exhibition. I also want to express the museum's appreciation to UW Publications, especially to Earl Madden for the design and to Linda Kietzer for coordinating production.

We also want to acknowledge the following people who worked on tree fabrication and putting the show together in Richard Artschwager's studio: Franz Buzawa, Christine Collins, Chris Freeman, Tom George, Jim Gowan, Tenjin Ikeda, Andrew Kennedy, Deidre Mahony, Bruno Musso, Neal Noble, An Pham, Jennifer Reese, Todd Richmond, Lisa Ruyter, Max Scott, Frieda Serrano, Ingrid Schaffner, and Alan Ulrich.

Finally, saving the last as a place of highest honor, I wish to express the museum's sincerest appreciation to the artist himself, Richard Artschwager, whose creative genius made it all possible. *Generations* is truly a remarkable work of art. Thank you.

Russell Panczenko
Director of the Elvehjem Museum of Art
October 1991

Richard Artschwager:
A New Overview

In the process of identifying an artist and his work, we need to focus on the images and historical references that reflect the subject and anticipate the resemblances. This approach is highly fertile in the sense that the mirrorlike kinship between present and past is a possible extension of the space in which the artist lengthens his shadow. For the writer this is a way of insinuating himself into an image to get as close to it as he can, thereby entering the labyrinth of art history. It is a search for interactions and interweavings in order to make the artist surface from the stream of time, to reflect other things and also himself.

In Richard Artschwager's oeuvre, fragments emerge and rise from the depths of history and the archaeology of its images. These fragments speak of an energy that flows over the powerful nuclei of the baroque and then of surrealism; they speak of painterly practices and iconic methods that evoke Rubens and Magritte, two figures who, though almost antipodean, can nevertheless be linked directly and diversely to Richard Artschwager.

The mention of the baroque may sound perhaps farfetched, but we can ascertain numerous similarities by revealing the respective ways of thinking. During the seventeenth century, the language of art and architecture concentrated on bizarreness in forms and surfaces—a feature allowing verity to turn into verisimilitude and reality into fantasy. The artistic creations of that era aimed at energizing the world of illusion. The imagination rejected all ''shalts'' and ''shalt nots,'' and the ideal of art was to embrace sculpture and architecture, drawing and painting. To do so, the art had to use technology and resolve problems of construction. It thus refused to break with pure practice, both concrete and manual; indeed it reemphasized mechanics and craftsmanship.

This interest in transforming material without intellectual mediation is at the very heart of the baroque heresy. By spurning ideal forms in favor of tactile and sensual constructions, whose external environments were opulent and unsettling, the artist not only established the freedom of his imagination, he also jumbled the real and the imaginary together, thereby launching a powerful dialectic between them. This (con)fusion created malaise by opening art to an expressive, but superficial assumption; it exalted the grandeur of sculptural masses and the monumentality of volumetric movements in terms of the logic and practice of construction, and it sang the praises of skin and voluptuousness in painting or sculpture. Bernini's draperies and Rubens's fur tunics added erotic bonds between clothes and bodies. Both artists

railed against the monotony and rationality of the cinquecento, disavowing any solid rapport with its primary geometry and developing an art ''from the depths'' of the festive and radiant visual senses.

There is not much difference between minimalism and Richard Artschwager's search for ''vanity'' in his sculpture. In the search he favors exception over monotony, so that clothing and body (no matter whether natural or artificial) turn into a single sub-

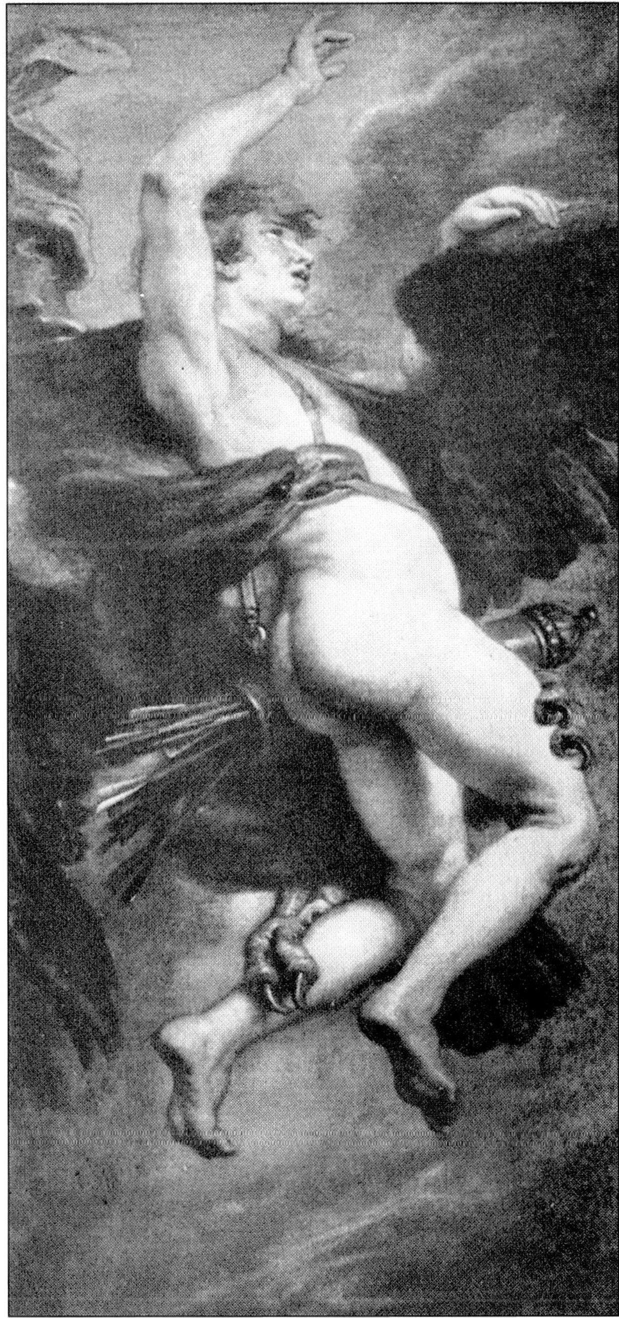

Fig. 1. Peter Paul Rubens, *Rape of Ganymede,* 1636–38, Museo del Prado, Madrid

stance, moving in the same mimetic dimension by imitating each other. We are reminded of baroque marquetries, which juxtapose diverse structures and colors, various grains, and contrasting decorations. Again it is Rubens who, with his approaches to dressing and undressing, tells about the superficial futility of skin, which is confused with painting, making both useless. Incarnating ideas in opulent female bodies with blooming complexions, Rubens tends to carry art toward a sensual communication that is antithetical to the rational geometric demonstrations of the preceding era. He thus works on the passion of life, on the things and images perceived by the senses.

Hence, art cannot place itself above or below experience. Instead, it must operate on the osmosis between subject and object. It cannot be cold or ascetic, it has to renounce ideas that are ''superior'' to others and identify with itself by showing the subject in terms of the object. It is no longer enough for art to understand and reason; it has to arouse the passions and the emotions. The pictorial or sculptural space is not blank; instead, being jampacked with phenomena and manifestations, it tends to seduce the viewer. To include all aspects of the senses, art must also call upon technology, which is why the baroque was interested in all possibilities of technology, transforming it into production by artisans of uninhibited virtuosity. Hence, as in Rubens's huge depiction of *The Rape of Ganymede* (1636–38, fig. 1), or Antaeus and Hercules, furious waves of sensational colors hurtle over the painted figures, creating a double epidermis of human skin and canvas, or else whirlwind accumulations of volumetric masses swell up into changing sensual protuberances. At times, as in many of Rubens's paintings, the impasto brush strokes scurry across smooth, compact wooden surfaces to be glorified next to the poetry of forms, the technical refinement, capable of transforming the coat of paint into flesh and blood.

With an identical physical fusion of body and wood, albeit in reverse, Magritte caresses the painted skin in *Découverte* (Discovery, 1927, fig. 2). He too aims at feigning a nonexistent reality halfway between illusion and reality, body and object. He uses color and figure to venture into the enigma and mystery of an eerie and ambiguous double existence; he uses painting and technique to seduce the eye and, like Rubens, he seeks a courtly beauty that enhances the viewer's pleasure. He accepts the vertigo of mutating imaginary quality based on exchanges and cross-references, on uncertainty and responses. Every so often, he looks for an equivocal reflection between figure and word, thing and body, self and other. He extends life in images, uniting them by dissociating or dislocating them. His work is thus a

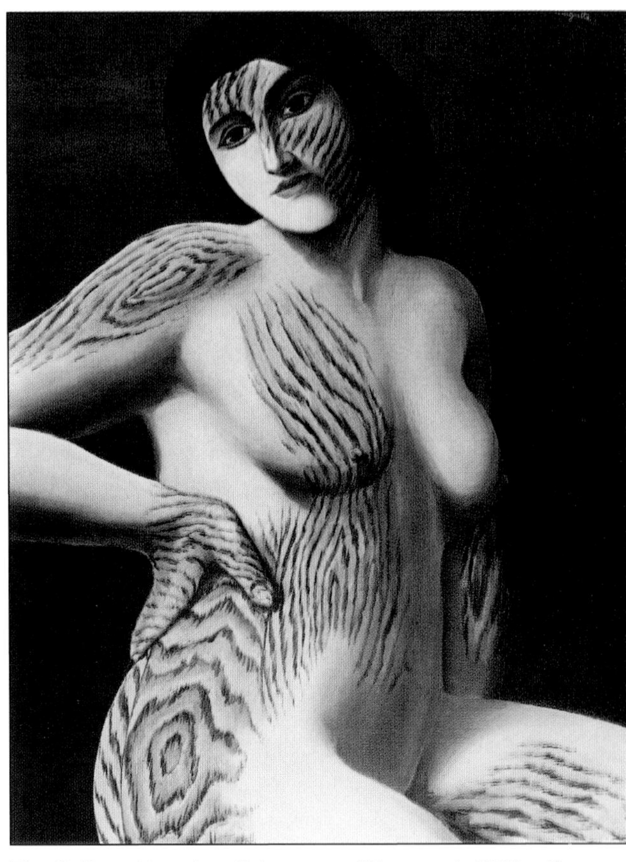

Fig. 2. Rene Magritte, *Découverte (Discovery),* 1928, oil on canvas, 25 1/2 × 19 1/4 inches, collection of Louis Scutenaire

continuous awakening that produces mirages tied to an unstable light in which every object and every figure are ambiguous.

Both Rubens and Magritte work with excess, metamorphosing skins and hides, clothes and surfaces of objects, making them offerings of fantastic life. They are giants or sirens, mythological heroes or carrot-colored bottles, freely ''changing,'' but not anarchic, and certainly humorous—a panicky or sarcastic humor. For both the baroque artist and the surrealist, the depicted elements pass into one another in terms of sensual variabilities in which the differences between mythical and true, verisimilar and unreal are intermeshed. Illusion dominates, and painting, at the apex of its craftsmanship, turns into a false mirror and a gateway to mystery. In Magritte, it touches the nudes or the familiar human figures as well as everyday objects with total exchange of appearances.

An identical transitive and visual bewilderment, accompanied by great sensual pleasure—both baroque and surreal—can be found in Richard Artschwager, who, since 1962, has devoted himself to seeking a new enchantment of both artistic and functional objects. His search for fluidity between painting and sculpture, between architecture and decoration has been highly singular, evolving on its own, outside of any trend or movement in our historical era. His earliest sculptural objects—from *Counter* and *Portrait I* (1962, fig. 3) to *Swivel* (1963), *Table with Pink Tablecloth* (1964)—yanked apart the utilitarian connections of everyday objects, making simple and naive things fickle and embarrassing. Subtly alluding to surrealist humor, Artschwager changed the order of things, giving them new faces rescued from functional investigations.

In 1964 Artschwager created an enigmatic universe with the safety of the mass-media icons typical of pop art or the reduction to primary structures typical of minimalism. He stationed himself on their threshold, condemning the figure, whether volumetric or iconic, to uncertainty. His constructions had a metaphysical malaise (a subtle reference to Giorgio De Chirico's *I mobili nella valla,* 1927) due to the simultaneity of table and texture, portrait and mirror, painting and sculpture, mobility and immobility. When Artschwager began working on the uncertain and reversible space of the same texture, Formica or Cellotex, that constitutes the epidermis of his paintings and sculptures, his location was equidistant between pop and minimalism. He cut himself a ''nonplace'' (another mirage), which was the ''nonemptiness'' in Rubens and the ''mystery'' in Magritte. Toying with the meaning and meaningfulness of his sculpture/furniture, Artschwager occupied the interstice between paradox and rationality, identity and visual squandering, decorum and kitsch.

Minimalism huddled in the stylized concealment of forms, a process of exclusion and prophylaxis in regard to the décor, while pop art sublimated banality and the consumer image. Artschwager proposes to unite those two possibilities, using both in order to transcend them. He accepts pure forms and volumes, but ''recovers'' them with images, thus producing a smooth and integral continuity between diverse entities. He weaves together surface and varnish, volume and figure. He slips in gently between Donald Judd's serial cubes and Andy Warhol's Brillo boxes conjuring up the real sense of enigma in an object. Artschwager offers minimalism the envelope it lacks and pop art an inner reality. He makes both of them familiar.

Richard Artschwager makes volatile the consistence of things, dissipating the object into the nonconsistence of images. He solidifies transparencies when he imbues the Cellotex surfaces with photographic landscapes or still lifes clipped out of magazines or newspapers, from *Apartment House* (1964) to *Johnson Wax Building* (1974). Or else he imprisons the lightness of a chair in *Chair/Chair* (1965) or the flexibility of a keyboard in *Piano II* (1965–79). These are images hardened by the superstructurings of surfaces and volumes, which involve marbleized Formica, in brown and blue. The use of an artificial and industrial skin adds an equivocalness to sculptures or objects or furnishings, whereby the indifference to definitions is intentional. The magmatic connotation and the blend of decoration of the colored Formica already imply a bogus knowledge, an optical illusion. Artschwager denounces the deceptiveness of things and asks whether they are not more interesting

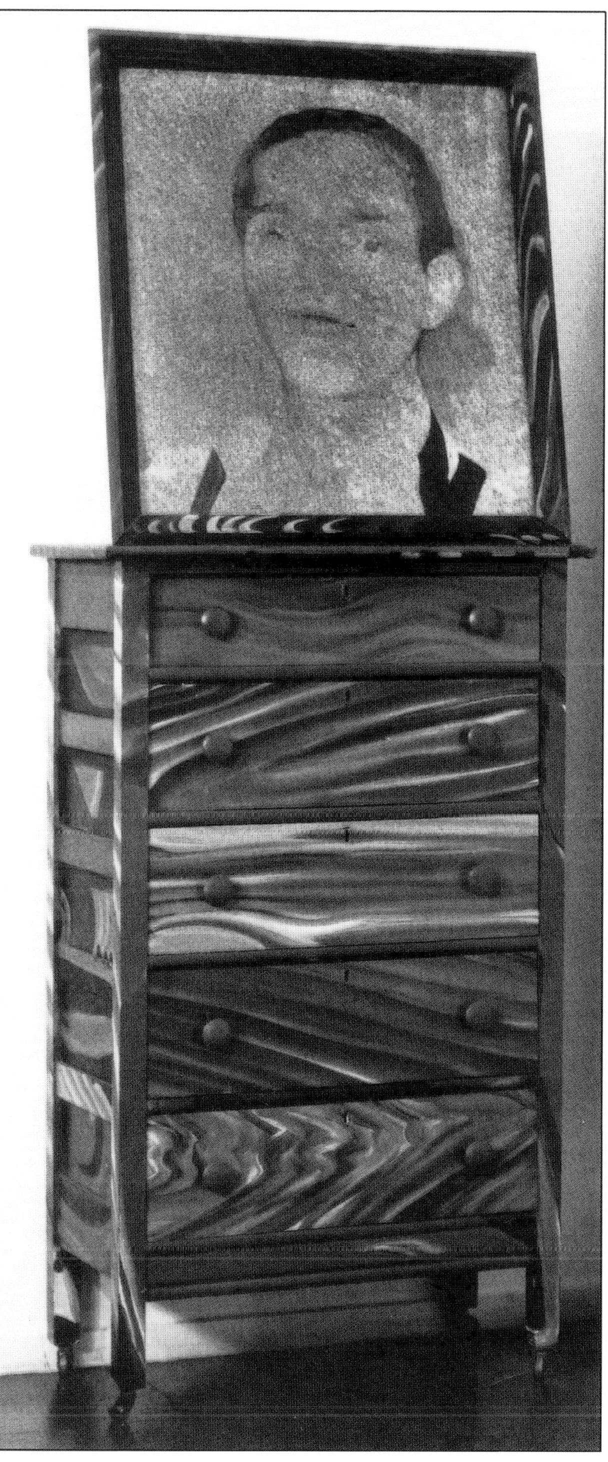

Fig. 3. Richard Artschwager, *Portrait I,* 1962, acrylic on wood and Celotex, 74 × 26 × 12 inches, collection of Kasper König

on the inside than on the outside. Thus the obvious appeal to the object is an initial seduction. He focuses on the inner body in its irritating state, as defined externally, thereby bringing its being to the surface—to use Freud's expression. The viewer is compelled to put up a defense against the deviance of the visible and to consider a possible internal secretion by the object: the pearl or the informative or communicative something that defines the relationships between outside and inside, surface and volume, reality and illusion, sculpture and painting, art and furniture.

Artschwager thus practices an art in which the signs of resemblance crisscross one another; he communicates the resemblance of the imaginary to the real; he abolishes the cleft between major arts and minor arts—sculpture and painting on the one hand and decoration and furniture on the other. He brings in an excess of visual energy in order to establish a communication between high culture and popular culture. By transcending the distinction between cultures or between substance and shadow, he categorically excludes the conception of a language as a supersensory or superlinguistic expression. Art shows itself, but possesses no truth whatsoever. Artschwager declares himself to be outside minimalist mysticism and pop populism. Like Duchamp, he conceives of art as a ''body,'' that is, as a mobile encumbrance in space: *Blp* (1968).

To grasp Artschwager's notion of sculpture, we have to quote him: ''Every time you make something, it is going to get in somebody's way. This will become more apparent in the 21st century'' (Richard Artschwager, Notebook, 13 March, 1982, unpublished).

Operating on the nondemarcation between things and between techniques, Artschwager continues the adventure of baroque and surrealism, extending them to the everyday world, to domestic life. He makes Magritte's mysterious consistence concrete and functional, joining it to the world of images, from *L'idée fixe* (1928, fig. 4) to *Sailors* (1966, fig. 5). Artschwager paints townscapes that become mobile or turn into practical sculptures such as *Pyramid* (1979); and he gives solidity to baroque brush strokes, transforming them into mirages of green Formica and Cellotex covered with black frottage in *D.M.B.R.T.W.* (1985). This involves both form and matter. In the form, representation is absolute: it neatly separates outlines of figures; while substance

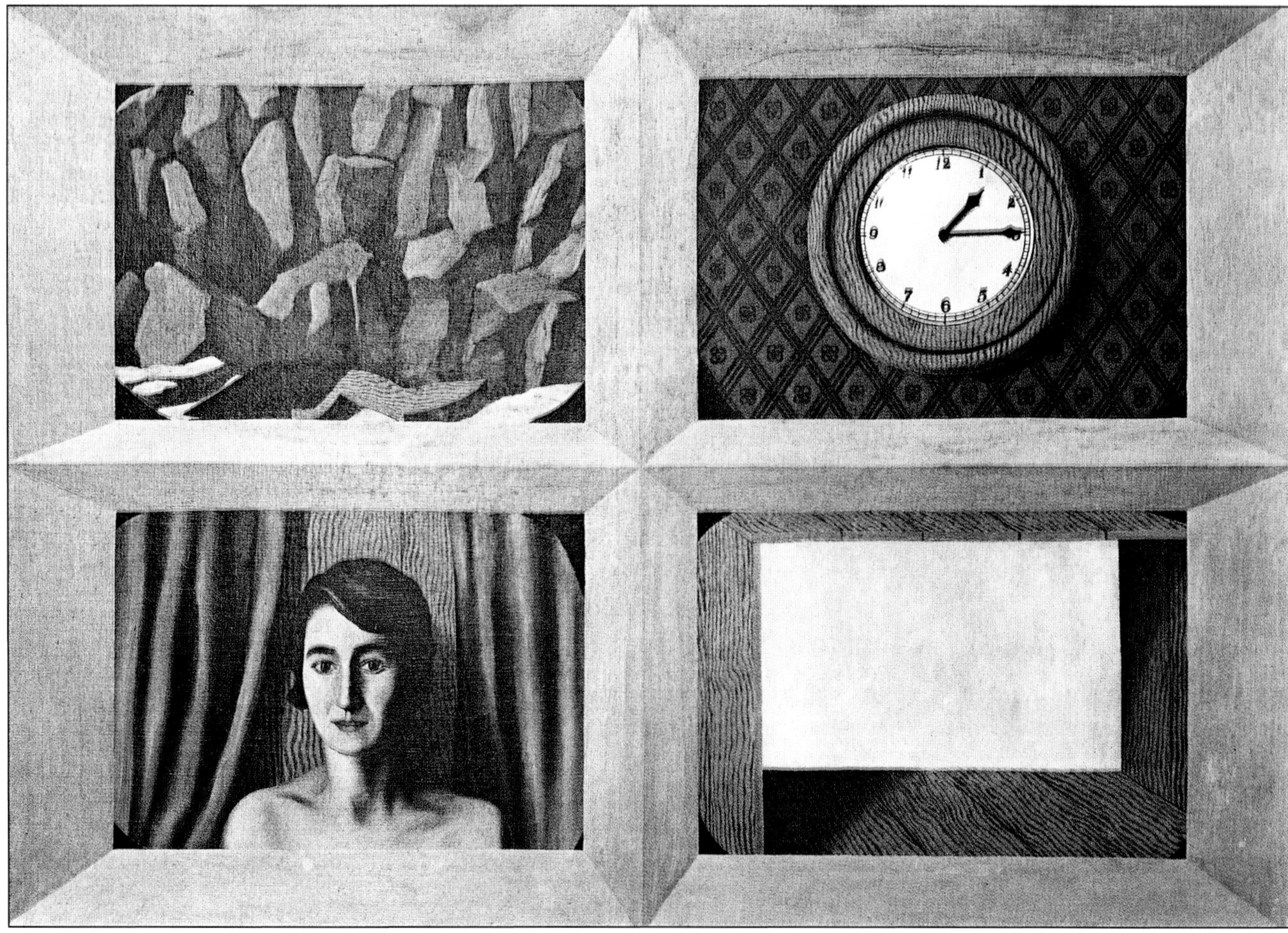

Fig. 4. Rene Magritte, *L'idée fixe,* 1928, oil on canvas, 31⁷/₈ × 45³/₄ inches, private collection

produces an identification of the two materials of the reflected reality. This clearly reveals how Artschwager, within the historical continuity, differs from Rubens, Magritte, and De Chirico.

Artschwager's images actually turn the values of the everyday landscape upside down. Not merely internal to the pictorial language, they overflow into the surroundings, becoming obstacles. Their consistence is their materiality, which is felicitous because it inseminates space with a harmonious but twofold condition: androgyny (again Duchamp). Thus, the oppositions belong to the past, art has become obvious, and décore undergoes experimentation. Now, both are ''in utility''—useless and useful at once, luxurious trades. And it is precisely technique and craftsmanship that make up the connection between baroque, surrealism, and Artschwager. All of them work on an artificial and, consciously, bourgeois reality in which the excessive affirmation of bodies, alliances, and objects explode. Exaggerated and extremist ensembles manage to become ''caricatural representations''—or rather ''with the humor'' of the icon and of the vision of the present world.

Artifice is a tool that is available to everyone; it accepts and selects any historical form to its own image. It rejects conflict, it stations itself wherever it (*Blp*) waxes enthusiastic over a happy or catastrophic image, devours it and enters into a symbiosis with it: *Destruction* (1966) and *Interior* (1973).

With respect to an art that tautologically affirms itself, whether aiming at the economic basis of the media or feeding on the microcosm of pure phenomenology, Artschwager places himself in a critical situation. It is hard for him to ascribe a disproportionate value to icons or volumes; by contrast, he has a growing interest in the notion of ''fetish'' as Freud used the term.

Participating in Freud's attitude, as the split in the ego, the fetish permits the coexistence of two positions that are incompatible in external reality: the recognition of that reality and its negation. It admits it as a value but denies it, thereby satisfying two contradictory demands. It transforms the useful into the useless. One could say that in *Low Overhead* (1984–85) and in *Organ of Cause and Effect III* (1986), the artist devotes himself to a more than functional international design, because he constructs an object more for its sign connotations and visual connotations than for its practical use. He circulates emotional and complex instruments in which the viewer can place a mental investment (again Rubens and Magritte), which elicits an individual response, so that the chosen object seems to depend greatly on the self-image of the doer and the viewer. The fetish indicates an investment of the libido in objects, the creation of an

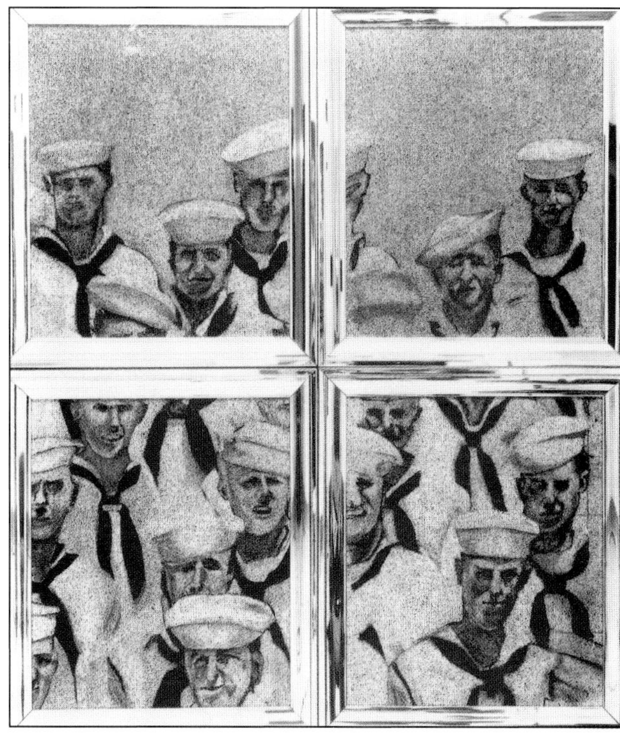

Fig. 5. Richard Artschwager, *Sailors,* 1966, acrylic on Celotex with metal frames, four panels: each 25 × 22 ¹/₂ inches

object signals the investment of the libido in the self-image. Consequently, Artschwager's works are halfway between artistic fetish and narcissistic object.

The imaginary combination of subject and object creates a familiar circle in which both feed on one another. This is a food that incorporates the eater. Hence, it comes as no surprise that many of Artschwager's paintings and sculptures deal with tables: *Three Dinners* (1984–85), *Dinner (Corner)* (1984–85), *Dinners* (1986), and *Double Dinner* (1988).

The food metaphor induces us to think in gustatory terms. It feeds a voluptuous density tied to physical and mental consumption. It mobilizes both skin and stomach. It evinces an internal pleasure of penetration and incorporation. Hence, not only is art beauty, it also signals both sensual and gustatory yearning and desire. It is a fruit that is seen, touched, and devoured in one fell swoop. It then follows that for Artschwager, painting or sculpture has to be taken to an explicitly carnal register. The contemplated bodies are nothing but surfaces to be covected. The eye becomes an instrument of distant possession; it approaches the prohibited flesh and allows an immediate sensual contact. Like Proust, Artschwager has a gift for the synesthesia of desire. He makes physical the invisible density of desire, disclosing it in an object.

The dream of the active inwardness of an object passes through the hard and soft stages of matter, which reacts to being invested, touched, and interro-

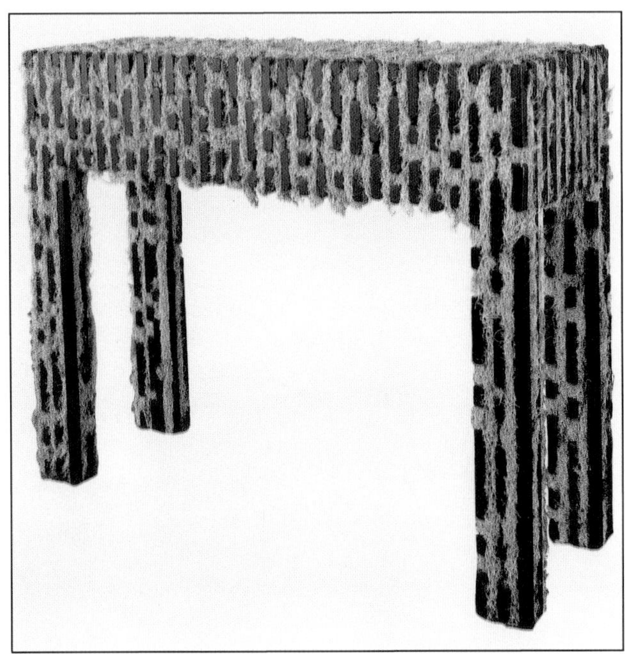

Fig. 6. Richard Artschwager, *Drawing of Table,* 1984–85, rubberized hair and wood, 36×46×15 inches, private collection

gated. *Blp* (1968), *Exclamation Point (Brush)* (1968), and *Drawing of Table* (1984–85, fig. 6) were executed in wood and rubberized hair or bristle in order to bring forth the rigid and tender, the caressing and caressable existence of object and subject. They introduce the pleasure of smoothness and mossiness.

The gratifying internalization and sensualization of domestic space find an antithetical complement in the cementification of the public space. The landscape, ranging from softness to hardness, is brusque, indeed almost aggressive. It is as if the loss of inward concentration led to a principle of crystallization and petrifaction in Artschwager's work. First in Münster, in 1987, for *Skulptur Projekte,* and then more recently in Santa Monica, California, and now in Madison, Wisconsin, the artist has introduced a hardness and weightiness, a sort of coagulation of the object: *Chair,* 1989, in granite. It almost seems as if density and consistence are being sought not in the opposition between superficial and profound, fluid and compact, but in the antinomy of private and public, transient and definitive, objectal and architectural.

Furthermore, sculpture per se, its configuration and its placement, tends toward a monumentality linked to the infinitely wider and phenomenologically unlimited range of the urban aspect. Nevertheless, Artschwager's monumental expression is neither universal nor idealistic; it thus rejects the feeling of grandeur and hides in the pleasure of the particular, the simple, and the everyday.

In Münster, Artschwager created Fahrradständermonumente (bicycle rack monuments), an aggrandizement of sculpture, in order to set up a ''monument'' to the bike rack. Thus, traditional monumental construction symbolizes not only the individual, but also the collective conscious. For Artschwager, the accumulation of values with which he intended to load his monument resided in his parking of his own bike: a gesture that was banal but, in Germany, highly cultural. The motive might seem nonheroic, but it was decidedly democratic, and the construction catalyzed the history and authority of common everyday actions. At the same time, since the monument was expressed in general images, what could be more general in Münster than biking or growing plants and flowers? Thus, this project was a further recovery of the ''minor'' degree of art, which Artschwager has not only invented, but also discovered, in relation to necessities and ritual uses of life and human and cultural ceremonies: *Tower III (Confessional)* (1980) and *Book II (Nike)* (1981).

And if Magritte states that ''painting is visible thinking,'' then Artschwager's oeuvre could be dubbed art as an action suspended between imagination and use, in which the latent force resides not so much in the mysterious and the unknown as in the used and the known. It is a borderline construction that creates passageways for bodies and objects to move through and settle. In Artschwager's art, emptiness is part of life; it aims at assimilating actions and things, at sitting at a table, or enabling us to kneel down, at reading or looking. And in this sense, Artschwager's sculpture has something catholic and sacrificial about it, not only because, in 1980 he was commissioned by the Catholic Church to do altars for naval vessels, but also because for him ''an object celebrates something.'' That is, absence is a symptom of presence, nonbeing is a sign of life. The image of the door in *Door}* (1983–84, fig. 7) and in *Low Overhead* (1984–85) suggests the passageway to the attainment of being, and here the passageway again consists of painting and sculpture. Likewise, *Sit-seated* (1991) vindicates the void not only as an empty place but also as the fecundating value of urban and public participation. Absence—again as in *Tower III (Confessional)*—is thus an index of authentic life in contrast with the illusion of the manifest object. Life that is not sacred or religious, but common and secular.

And, to conclude, a further analogy: when Arthur Artaud compares his writing and his directing to the visual arts, he says that his oeuvre is ''a mute theater, but it speaks much more than it would if it had a language to express itself.'' Thus Artschwager's interventions in the urban context are mute scenes. They occur in a climate of serene contempla-

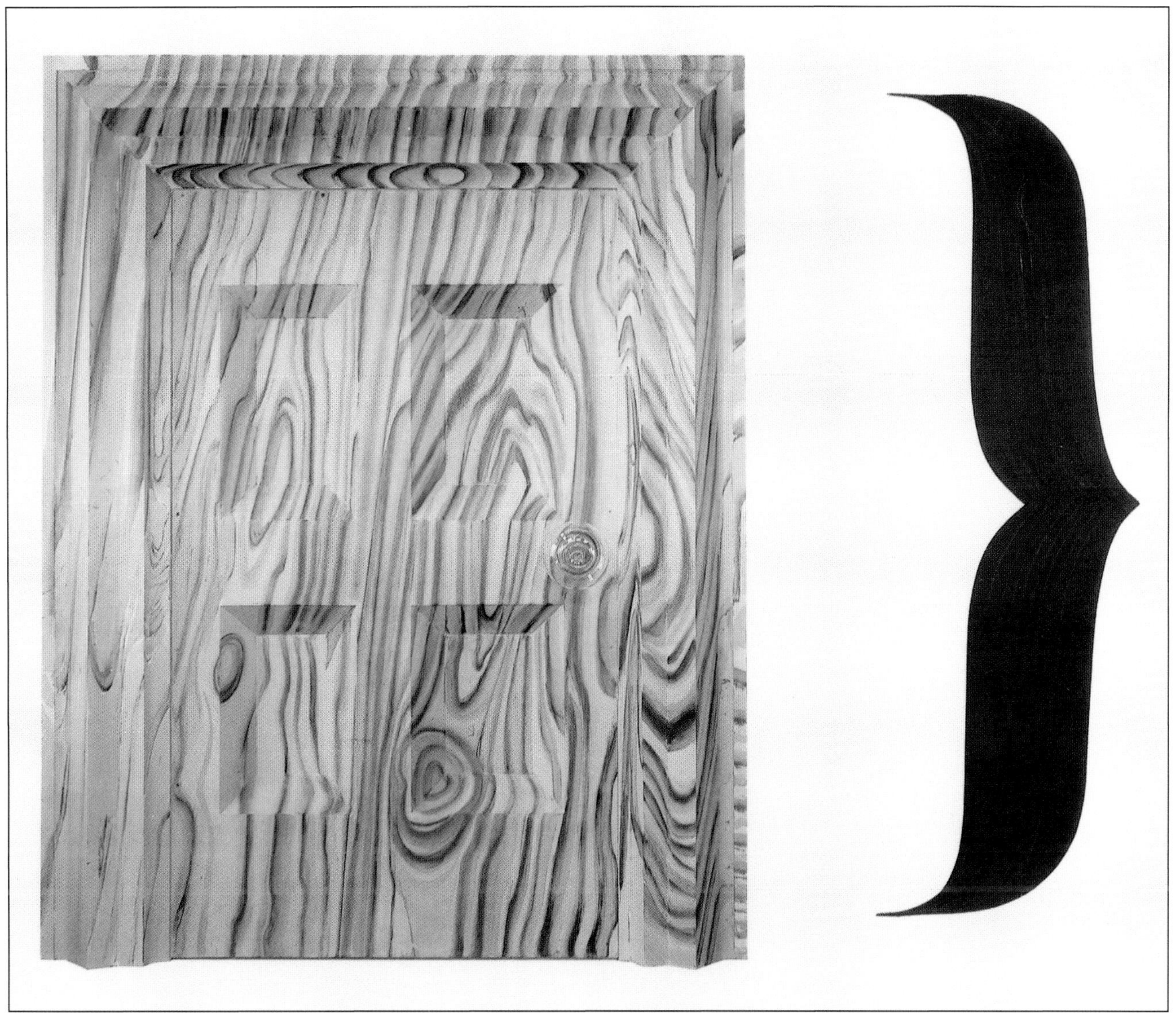

Fig. 7. Richard Artschwager, *Door}*, 1983–84, acrylic on wood and glass, two parts: door 81³/₄ × 65 × 9³/₄ inches, bracket 74¹/₄ × 25 × 1¹/₂ inches, collection of Martin Bernstein

tion. They include a negation of noisy and clamorous images and insist on silence, on waiting, on enigma. They do not intend to say much, but they contain details, signs, and figures waiting to be discovered, conquered, and acted upon. Simultaneously playing all scores of architecture and sculpture, decoration and painting in an ultimate montage, they are witnesses to and illuminated custodians of the ability to seduce and conquer.

Germano Celant
Curator of Contemporary Art
Solomon R. Guggenheim Museum
New York, August, 1991

Translated from the Italian by
Joachim Neugroschel © 1991, English translation

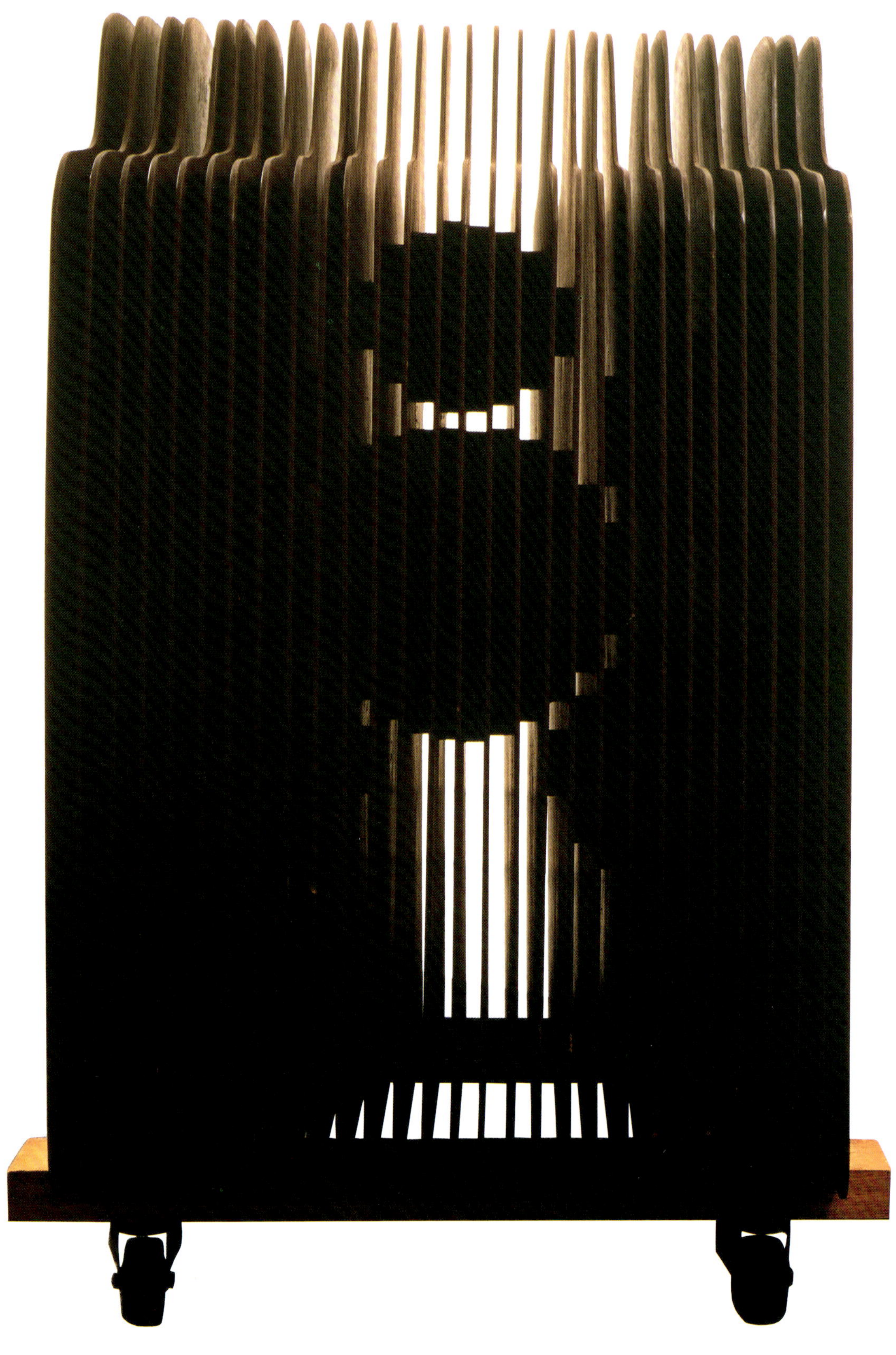

Gorilla, 1961–62
Acrylic on masonite, wood, and metal casters, 47 × 32 × 32 1/4 inches
Courtesy Kent Fine Art, Inc., New York

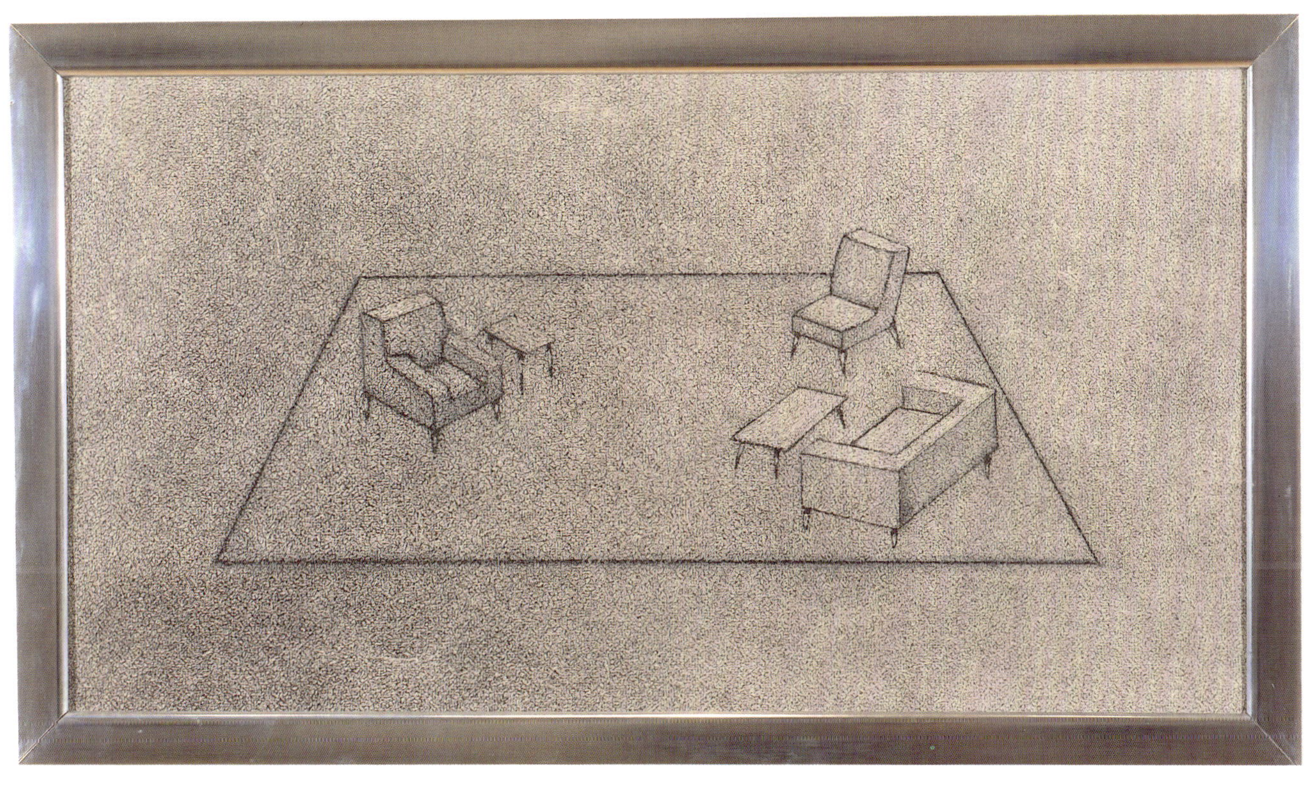

Chair, Chair, Sofa, Table, Table Rug, 1965
Acrylic on Celotex with metal frame, 23 1/8 × 41 1/8 inches
Collection of Jill Sussman, New York

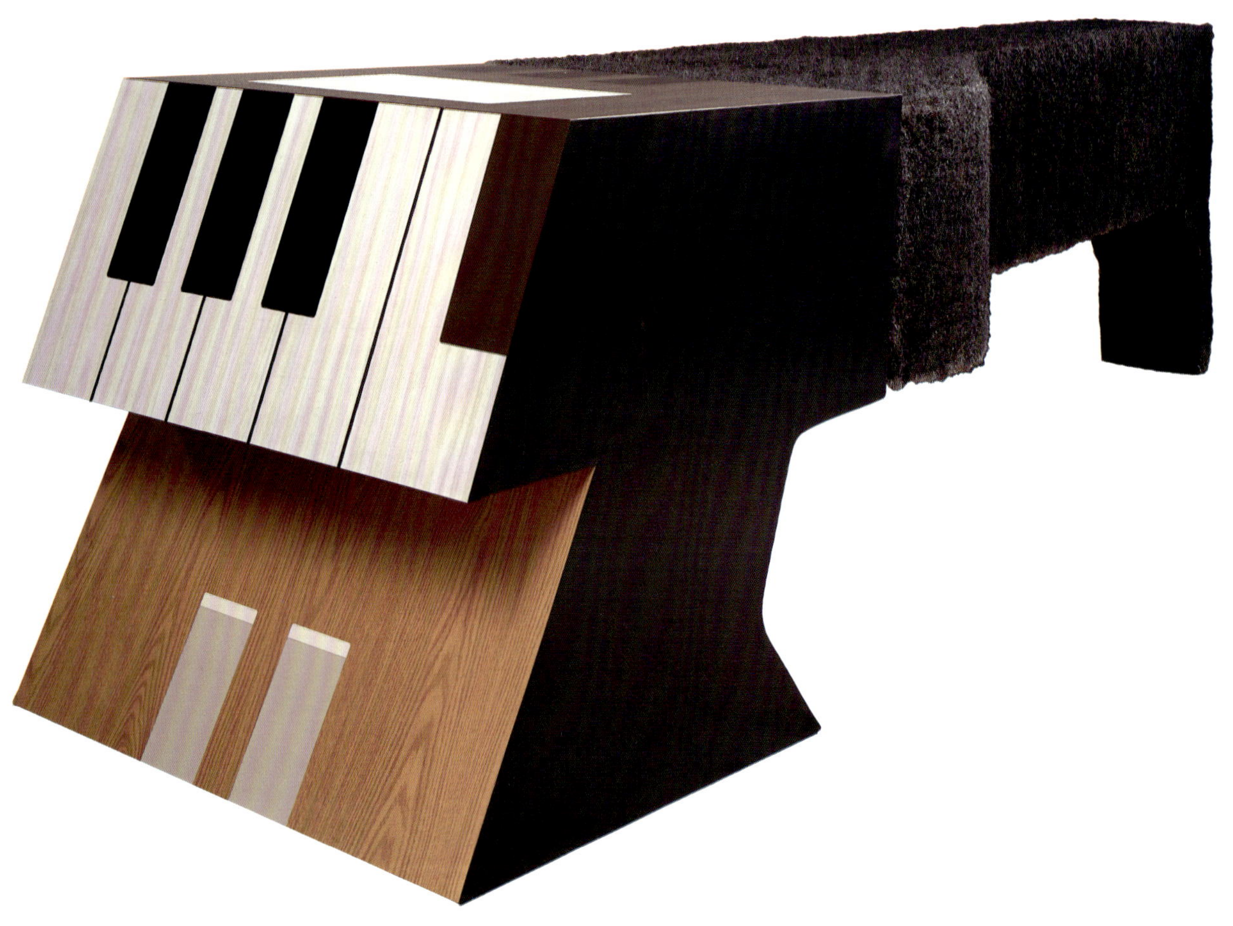

Piano II, 1965–79
Formica on wood with rubberized hair, 33^3/$_4$×34×130 inches
Courtesy Kent Fine Art, Inc., New York

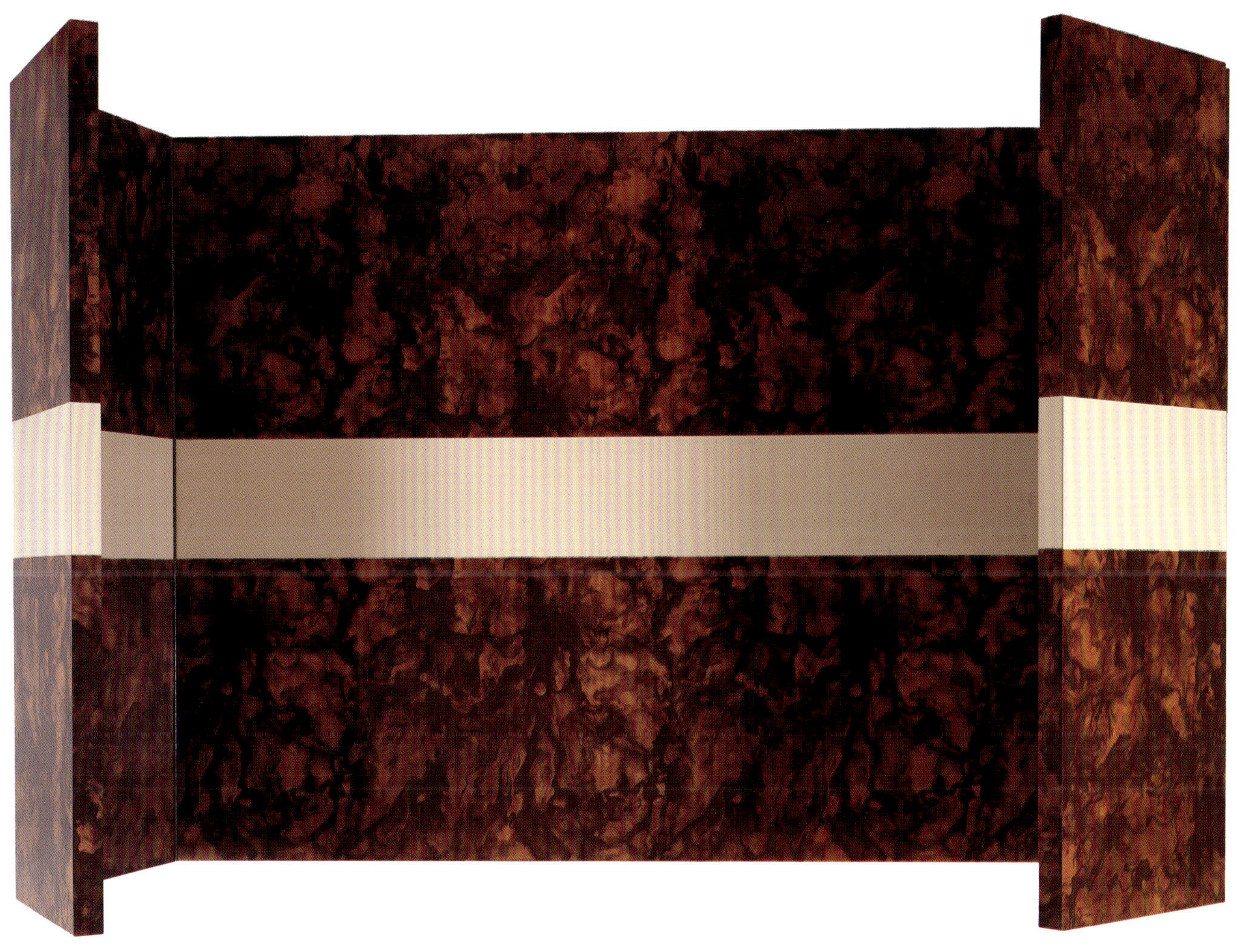

Faceted Syndrome, 1967
Formica on wood, 71¹/₂×191×5 inches
Collection of the Artist

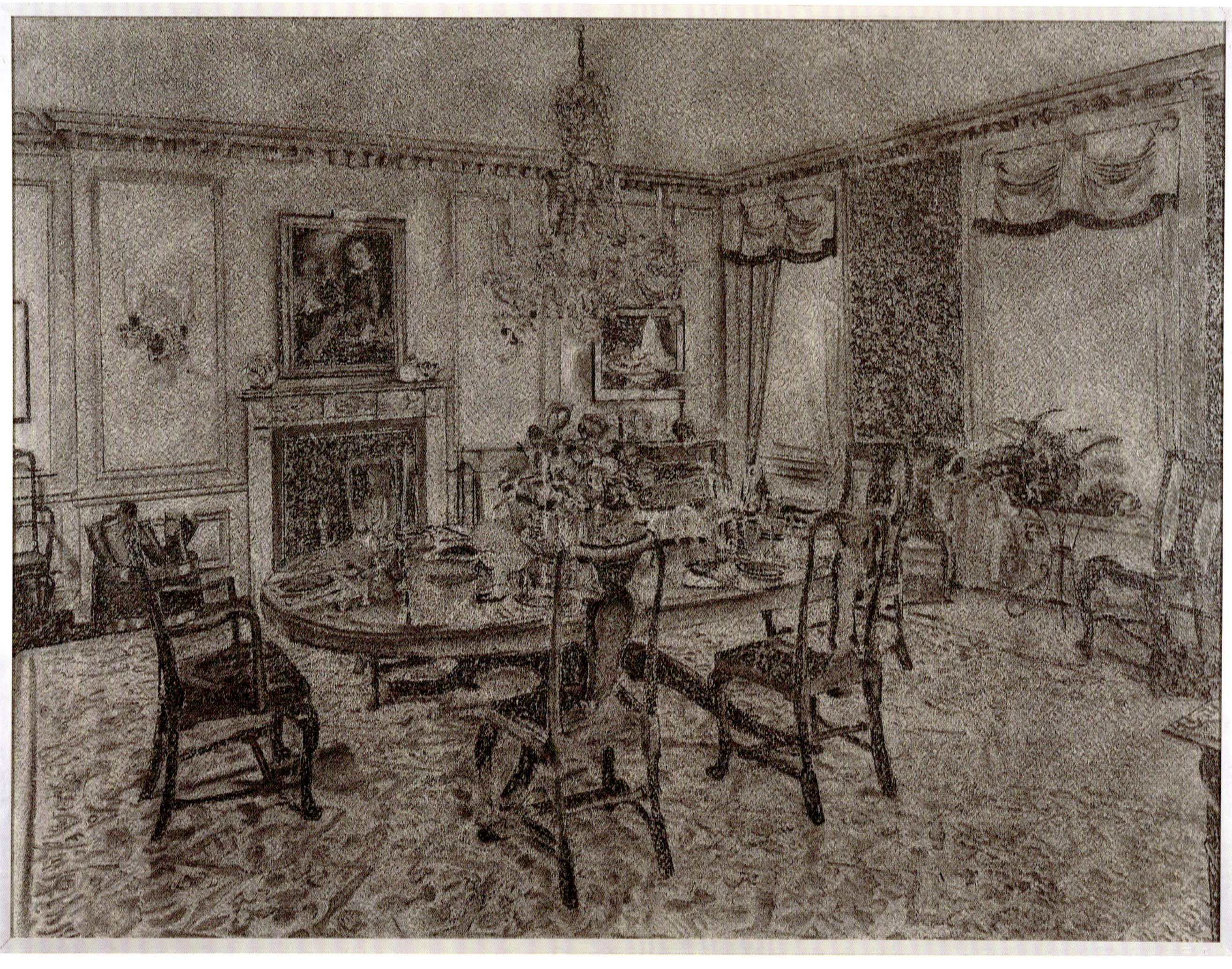

Polish Rider, 1970–71
Acrylic on Celotex, 45 1/4 × 61 3/8 inches
Collection of Museum of Contemporary Art, Chicago
Gift of Mrs. Robert B. Mayer

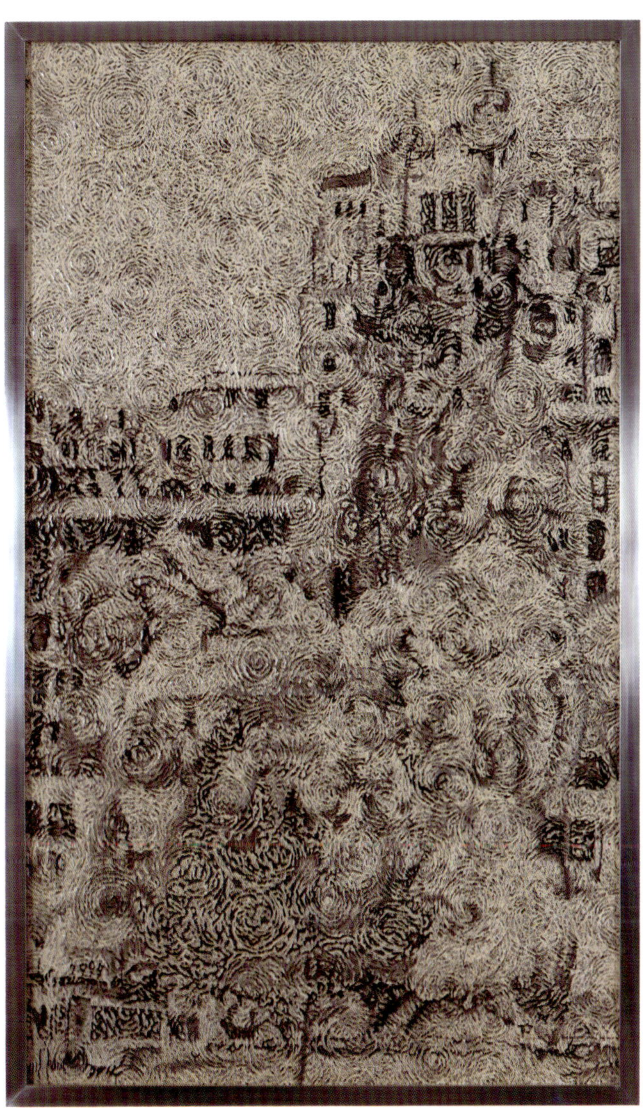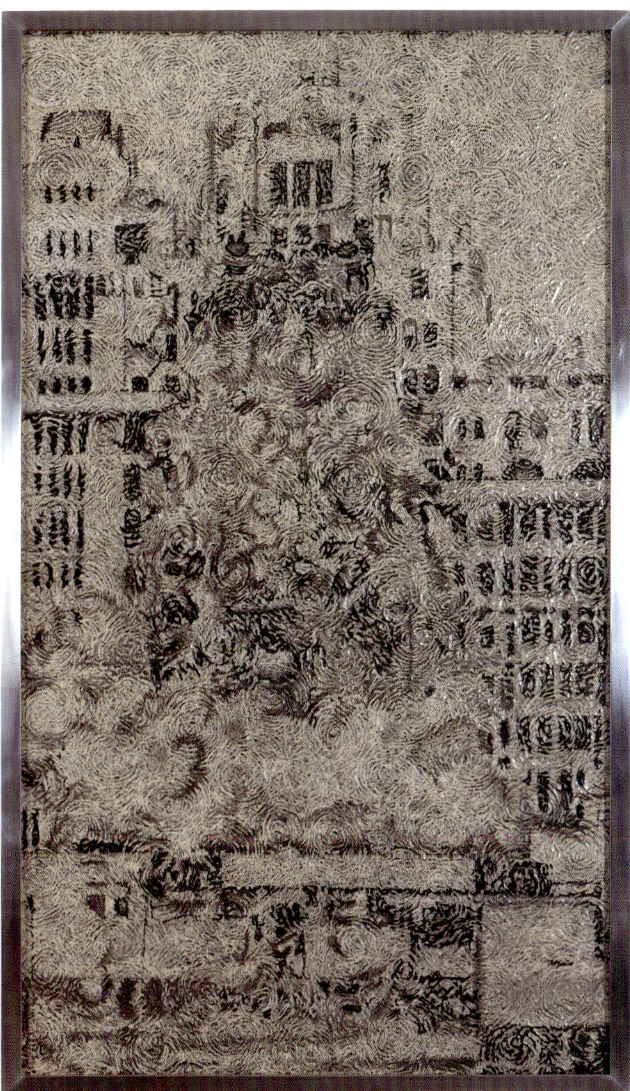

Destruction V, 1972
Acrylic on Celotex, each panel, 39³/₄ × 23¹/₈ inches
Collection of Eli and Edythe L. Broad

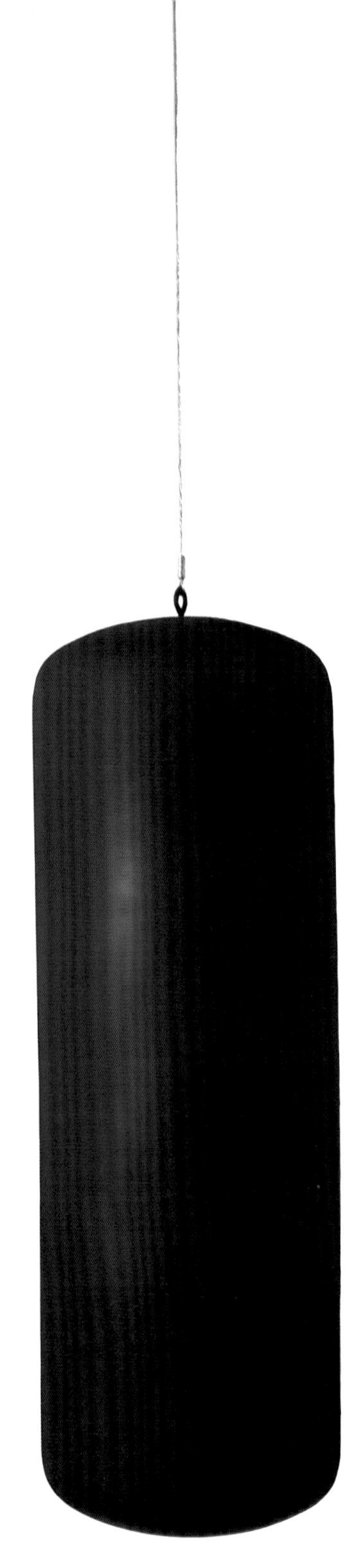

Blp (Metal), 1972
Enamel on steel, 44 inches×14 inches diameter
Collection of the Artist

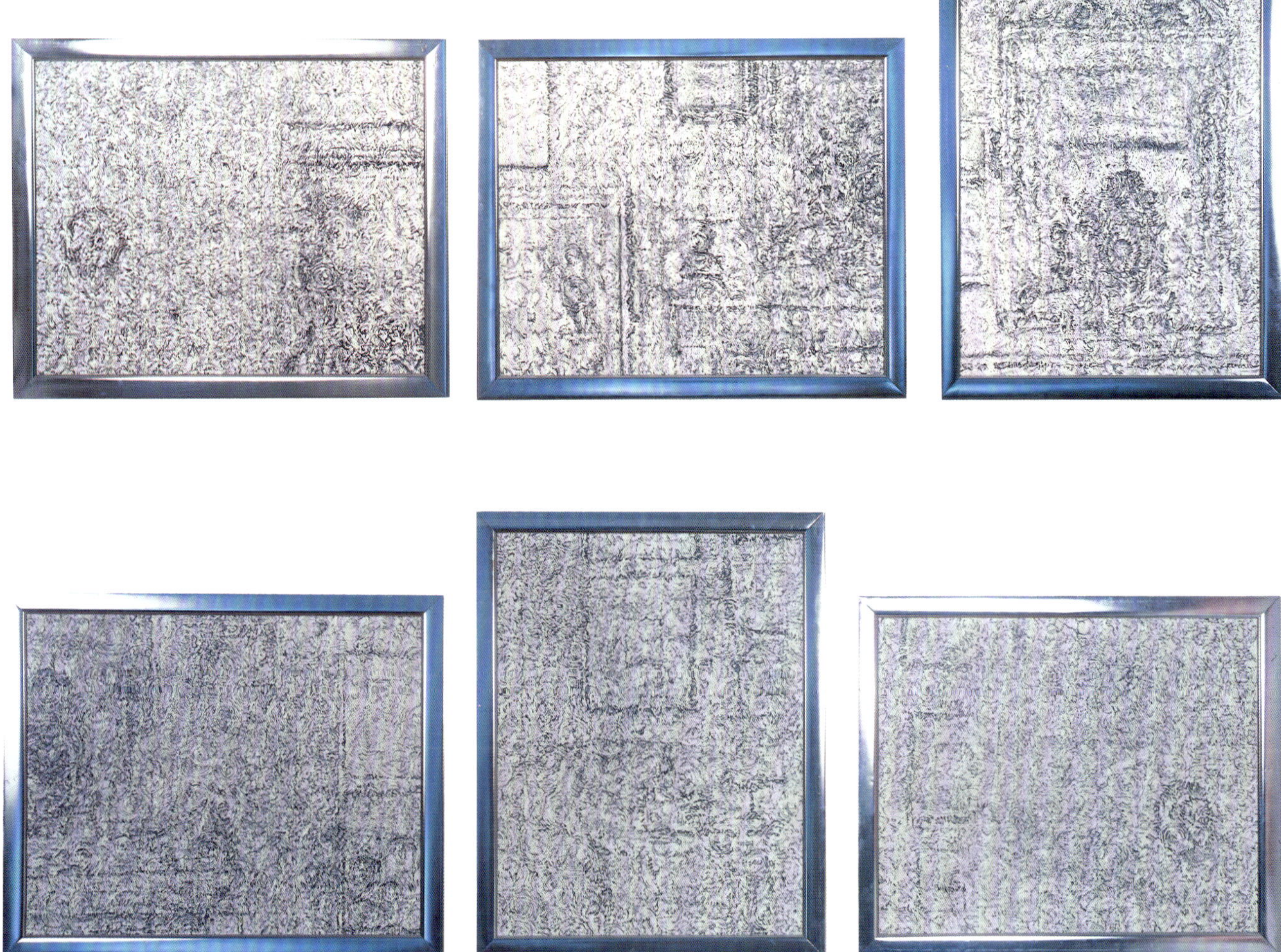

Doors II, 1973
Acrylic on Celotex, six panels 32 × 26 inches and 26 × 32 inches
Courtesy Kent Fine Art, Inc., New York

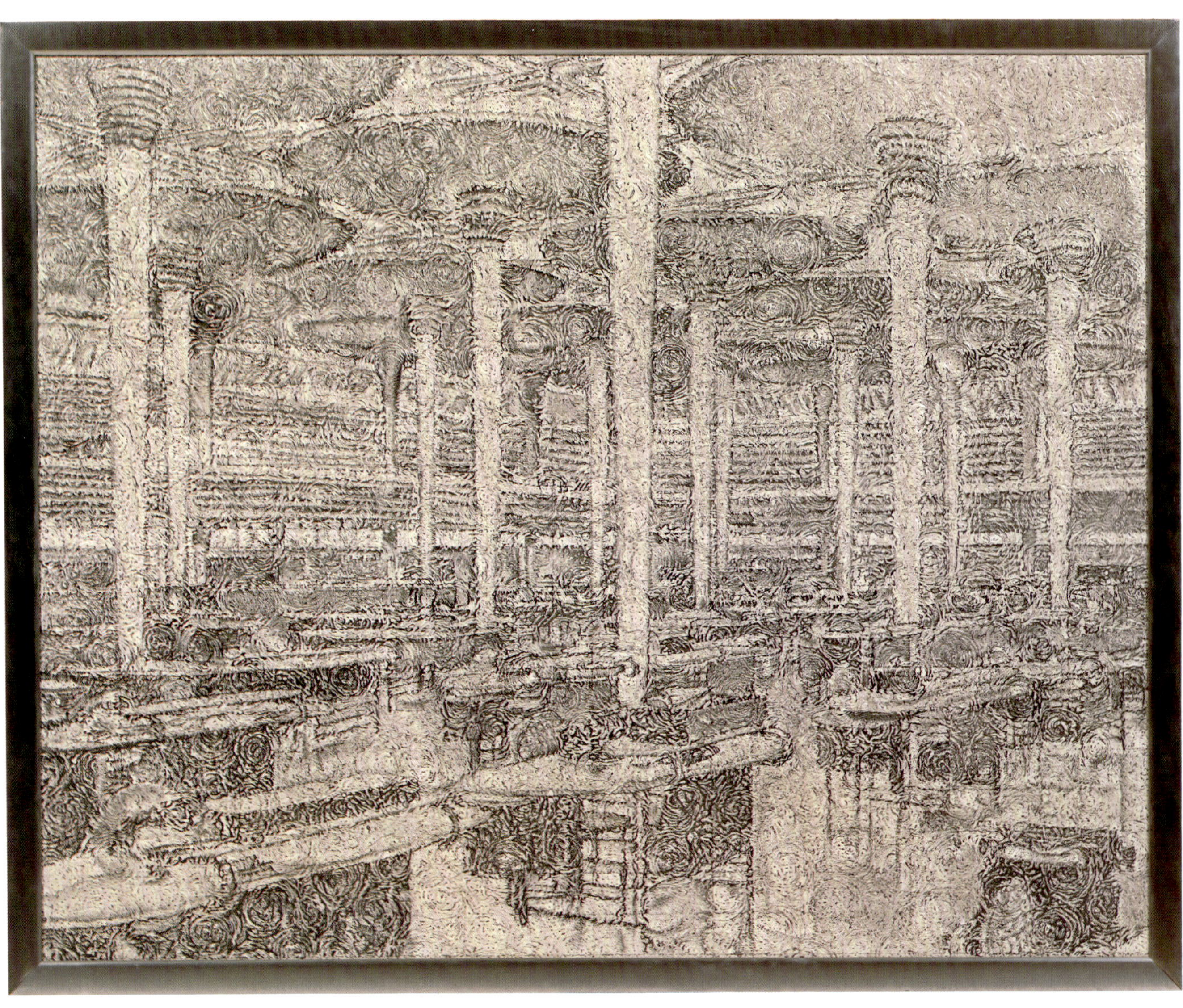

Johnson Wax Building, 1974
Acrylic on Celotex, $47\,5/8 \times 59\,1/2$ inches
Collection of The Edward R. Broida Trust

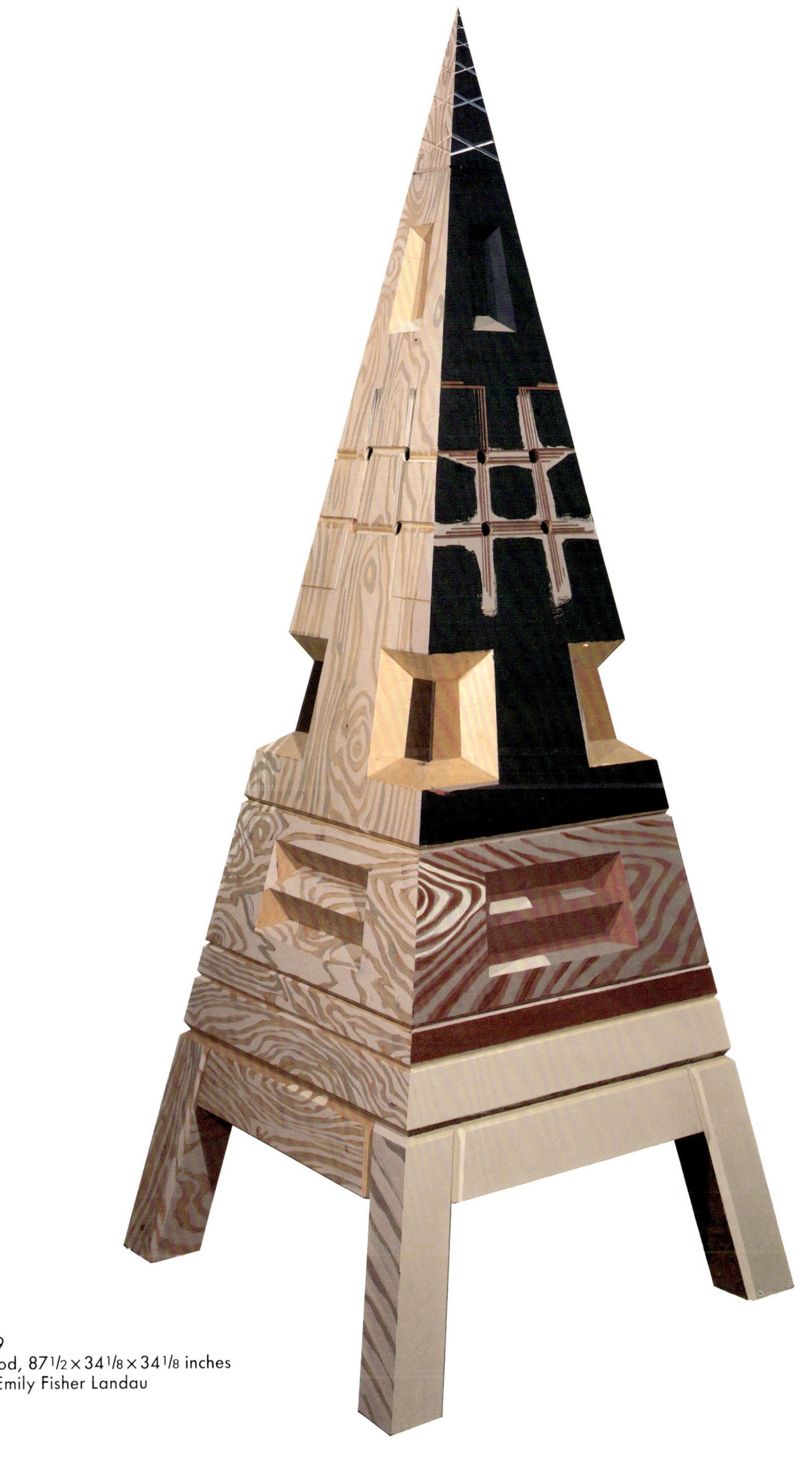

Pyramid, 1979
Acrylic on wood, 87 1/2 × 34 1/8 × 34 1/8 inches
Collection of Emily Fisher Landau

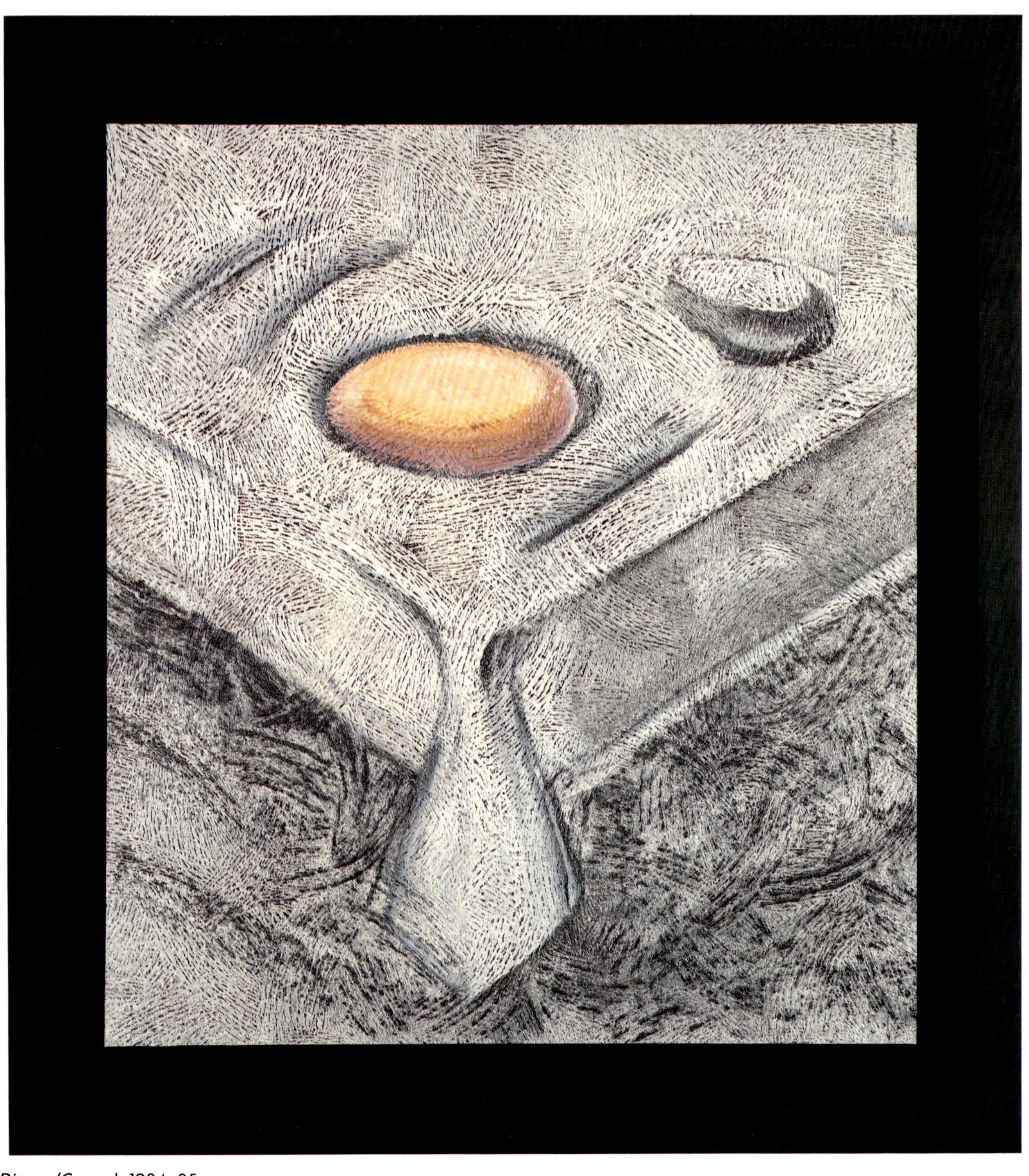

Dinner (Corner), 1984–85
Liquitex on Celotex, 30 × 27 1/2 × 3 inches
Collection of Patricia Brundage and William Copley

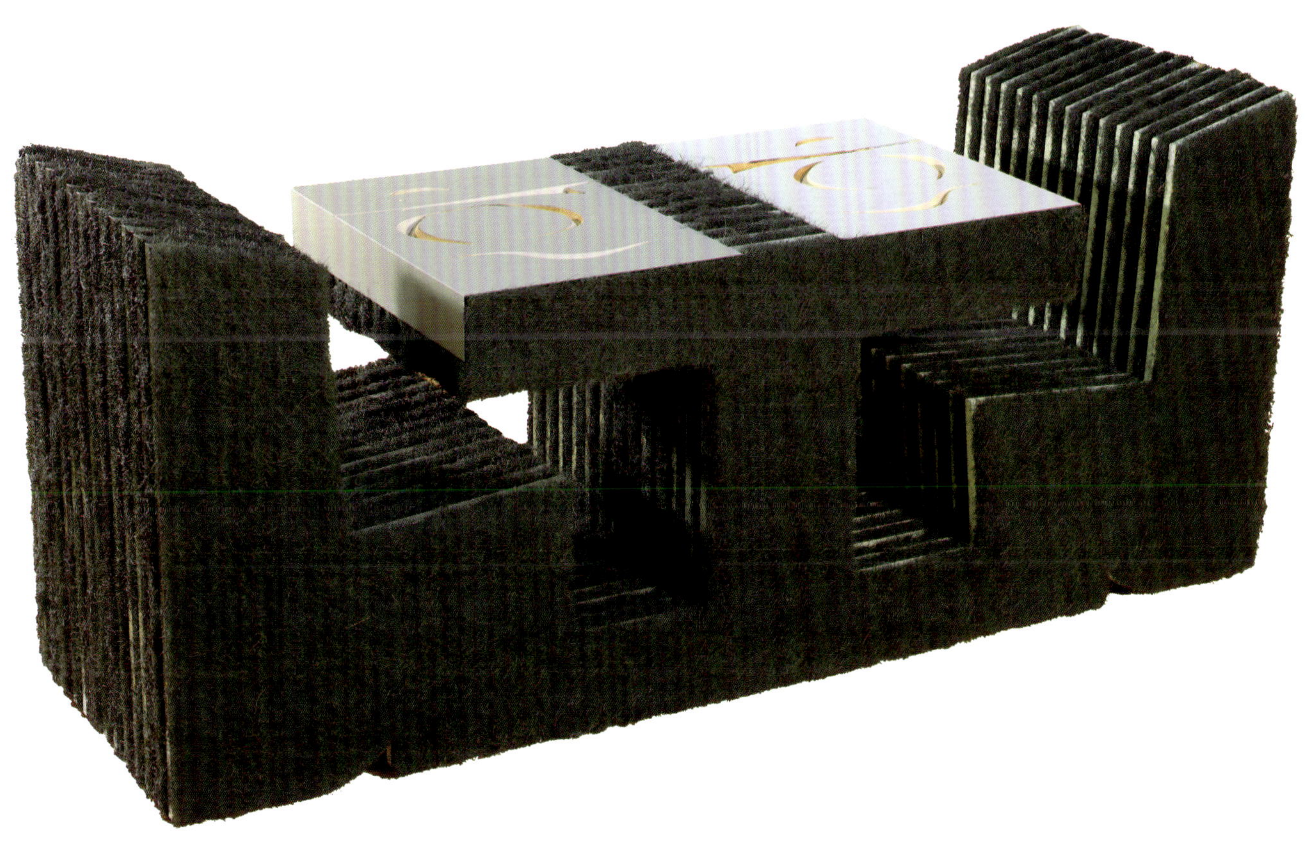

Double Dinner, 1988
Formica on wood, enamel on wood with rubberized hair,
35 1/2 × 27 × 85 inches
Collection of Illeana Sonnebend

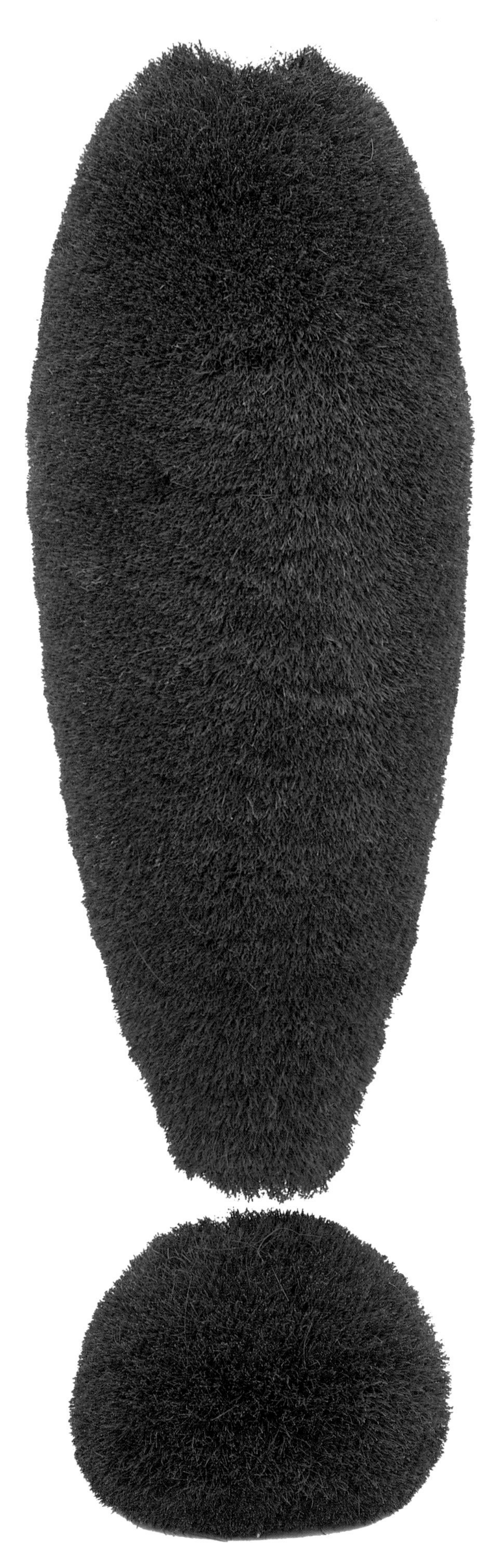

Exclamation Point (Brush), 1988
Wood and bristle, two parts: exclamation $5 \times 2^{1}/_{2} \times 2^{1}/_{2}$ feet,
dot 2 feet diameter
Courtesy of Leo Castelli Gallery, New York

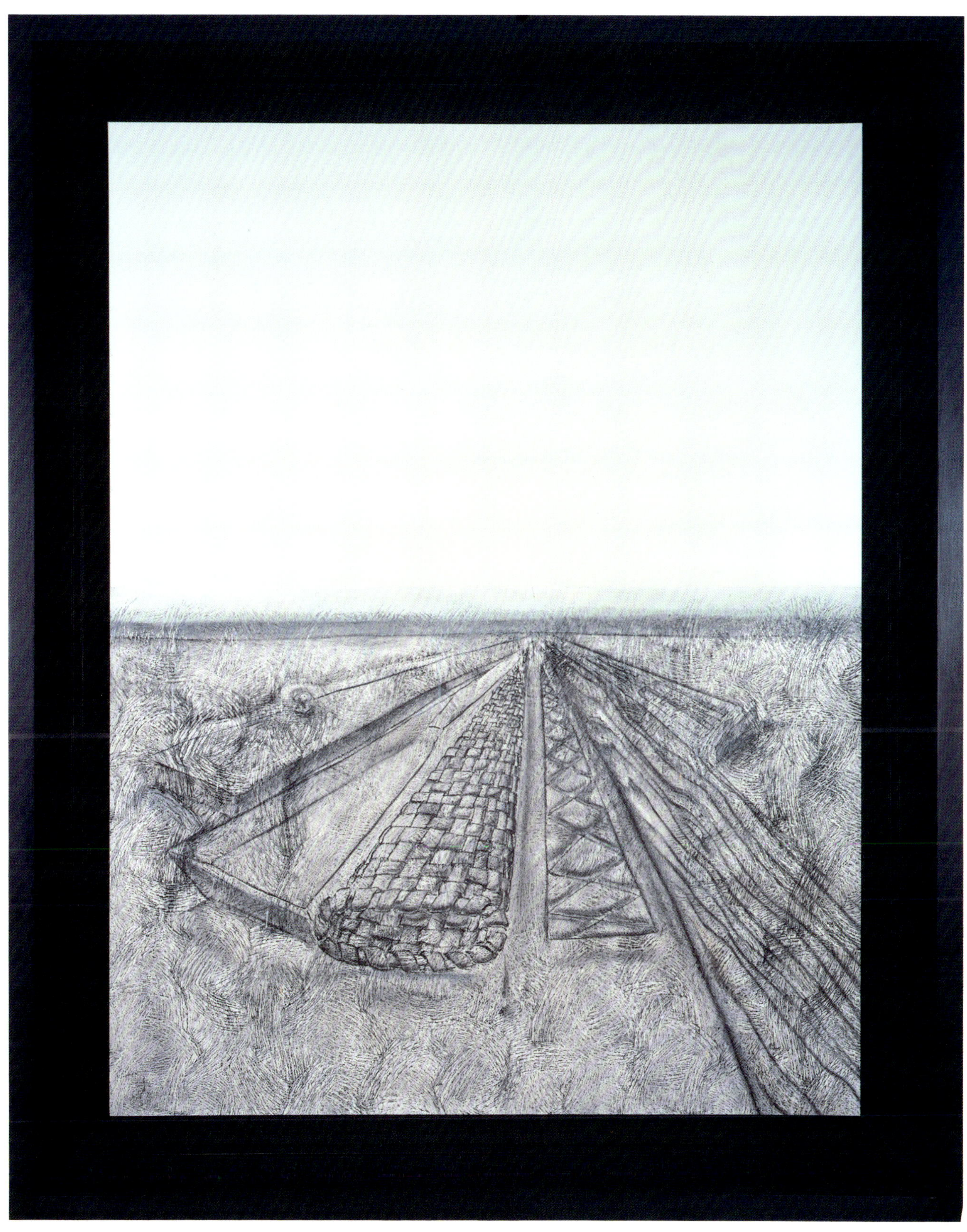

TWMDRB, 1988
Acrylic on Celotex and Formica on wood, 60 × 72 × 8 inches
Collection of the Artist

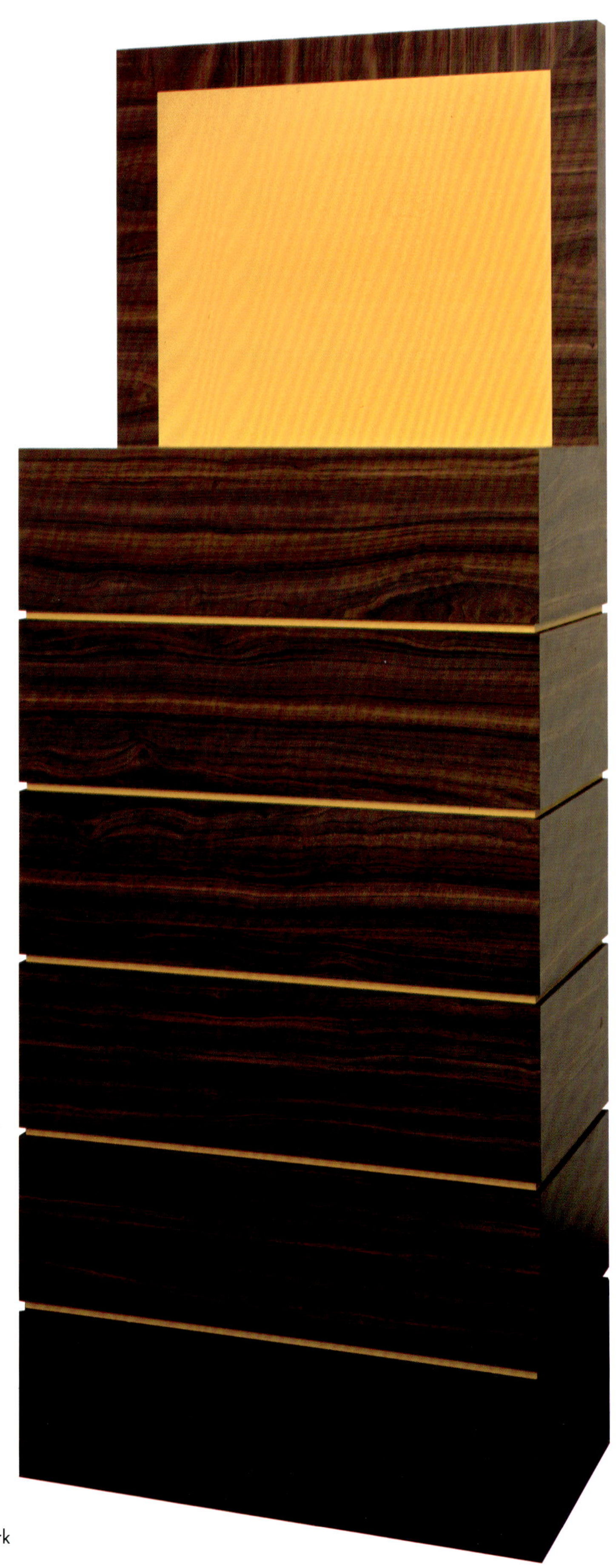

Portrait III, 1989
Formica on wood, 72 × 27¹/₄ × 13³/₄ inches
Courtesy of Rubin Spangle Gallery, New York

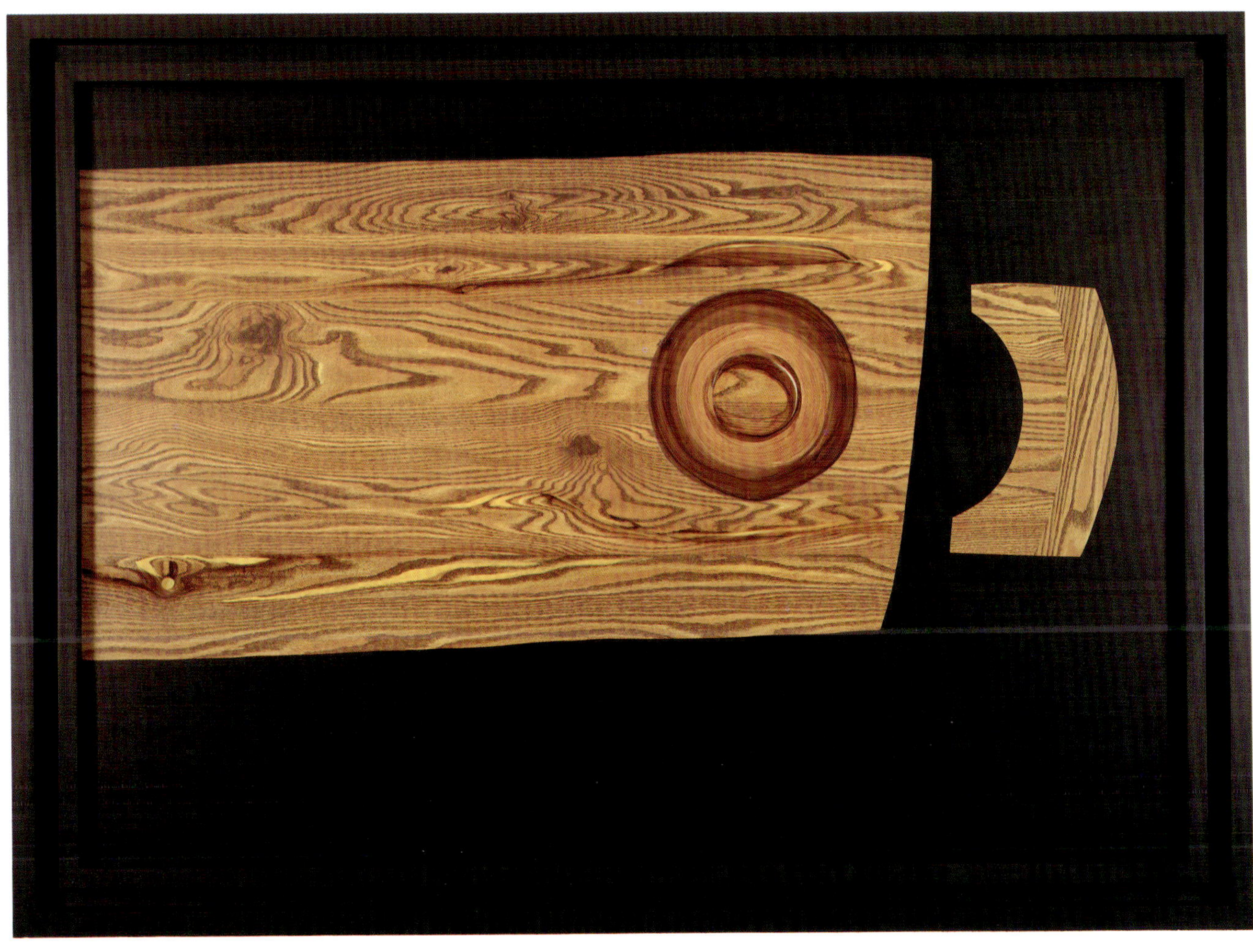

Sitting, 1990
Acrylic on Formica and wood, 50 × 68 × 4 1/2 inches
Collection of the Artist

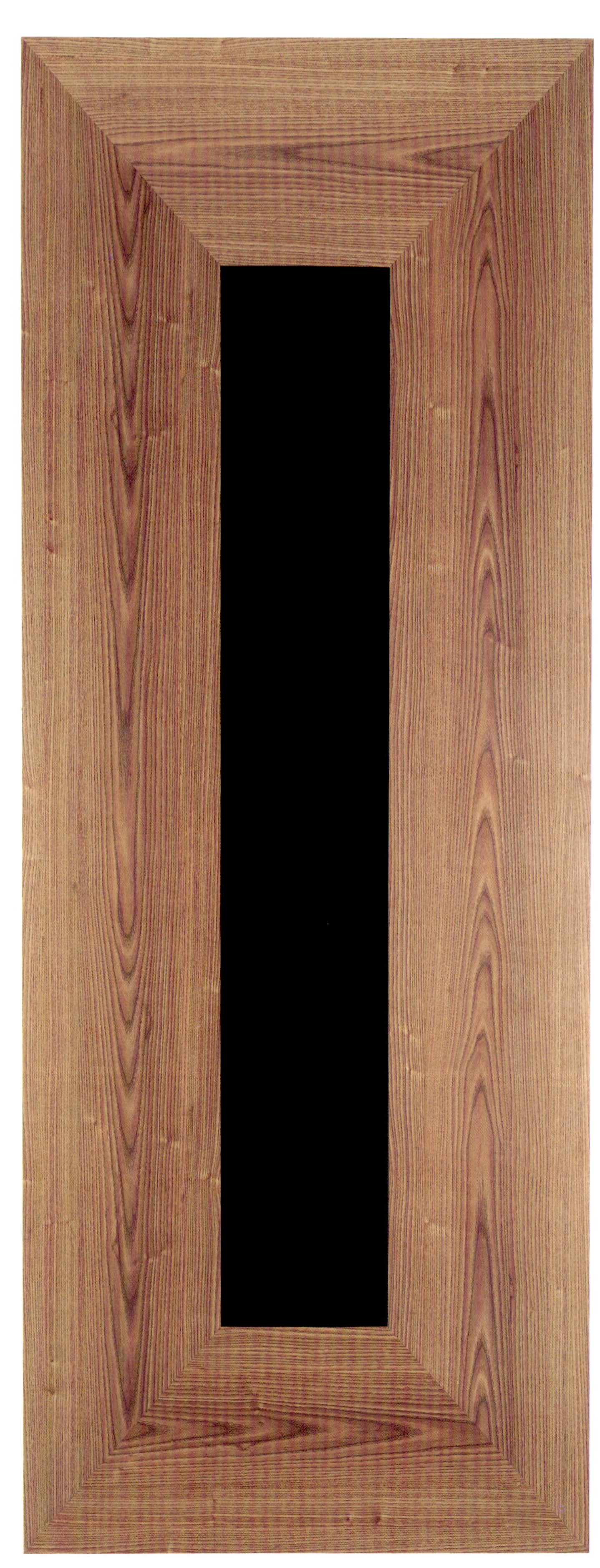

Mirror, 1991
Formica and enamel on wood, 87 × 33 1/2 inches
Collection of the Artist

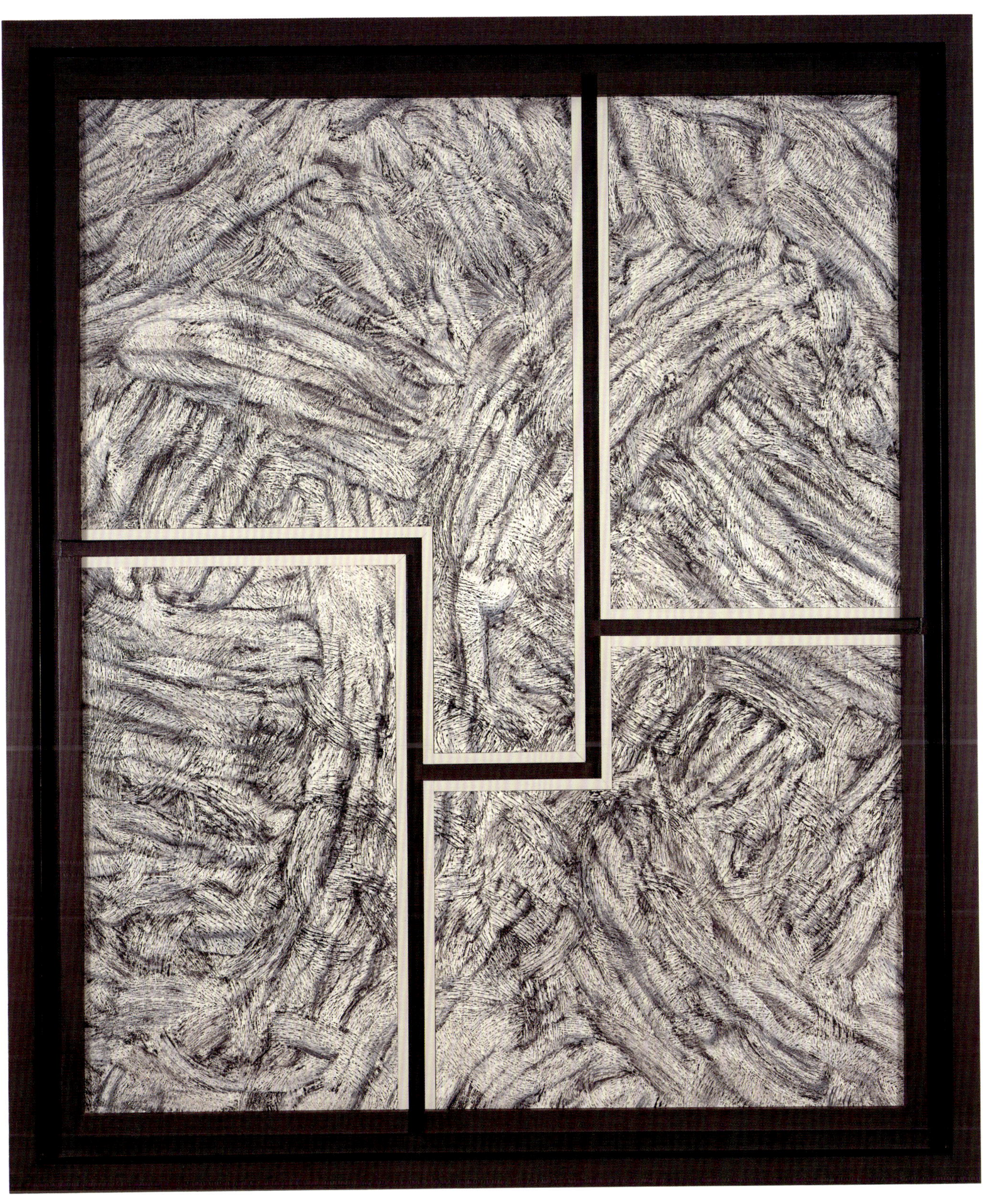

WEAVE/weave, 1991
Acrylic on Celotex, 48 × 60 × 5 inches
Collection of the Artist

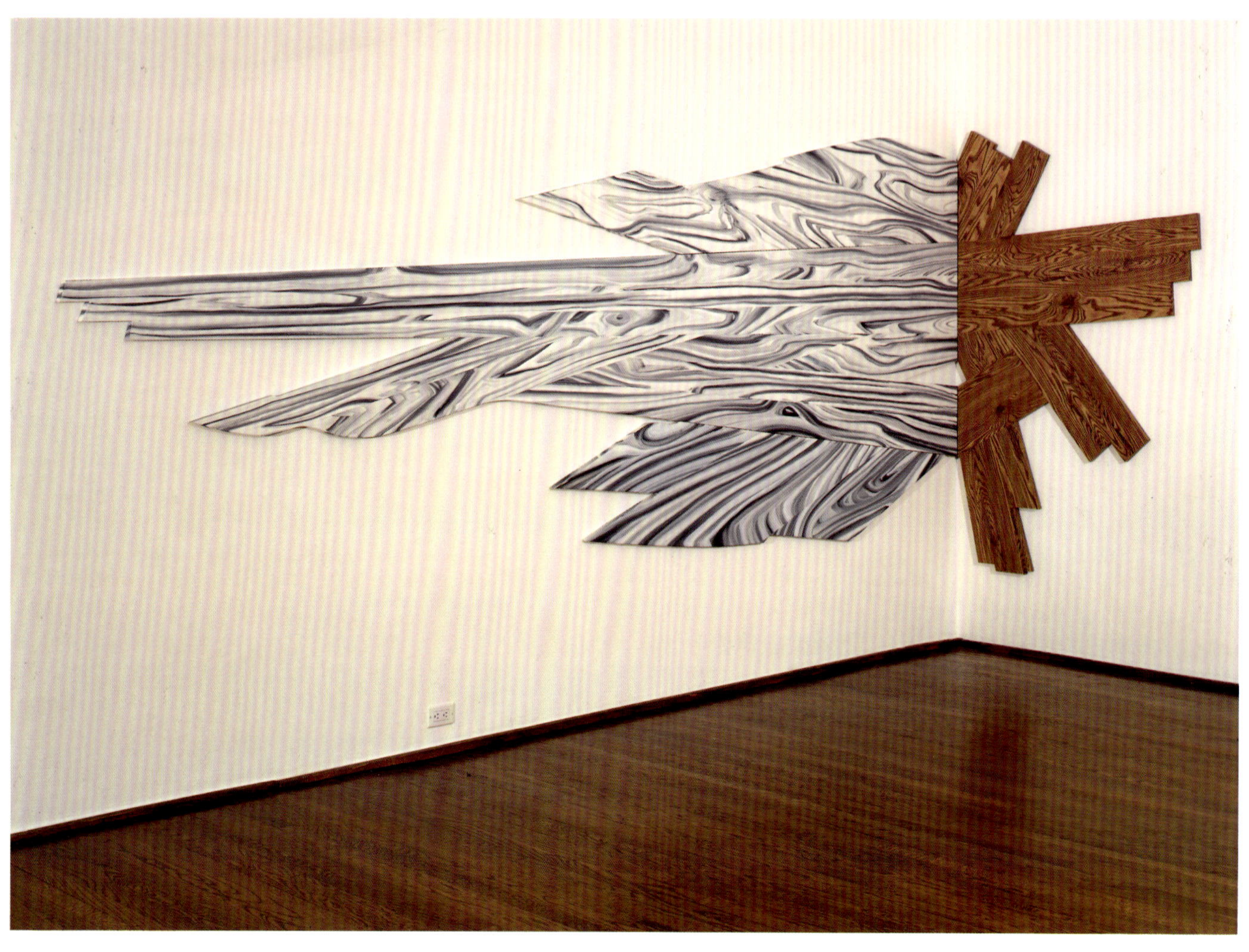

Journal II, 1991
Formica and acrylic on wood, two parts: left side
56 × 172 1/2 × 1 1/4 inches; right side 80 × 51 × 1 1/2 inches
Collection of the Artist

Richard Artschwager's Outdoor Commissions, 1982–91

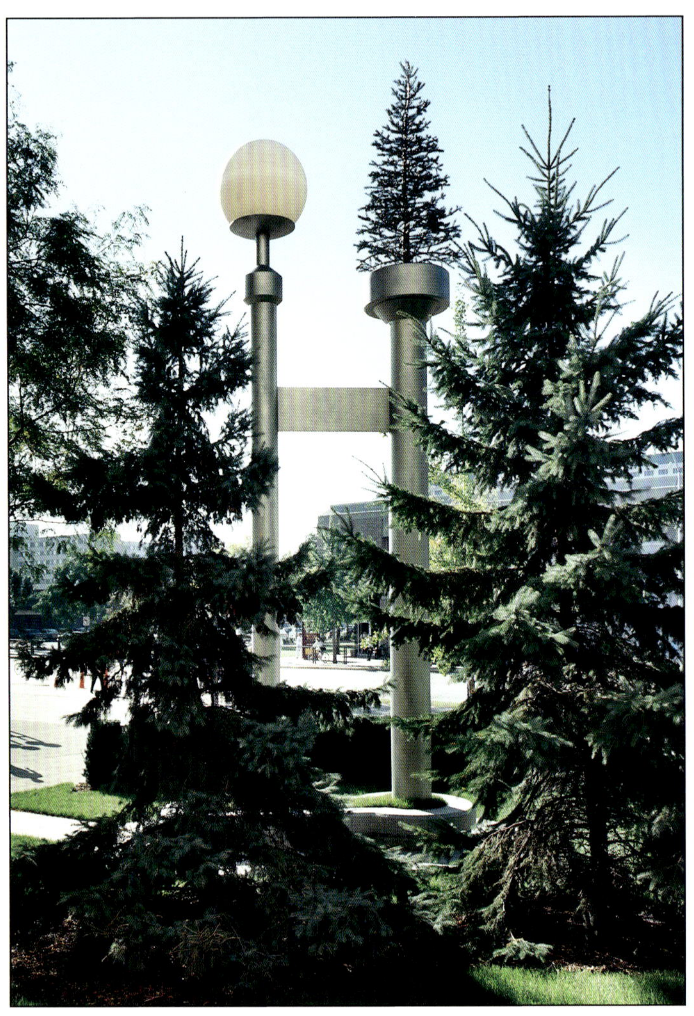 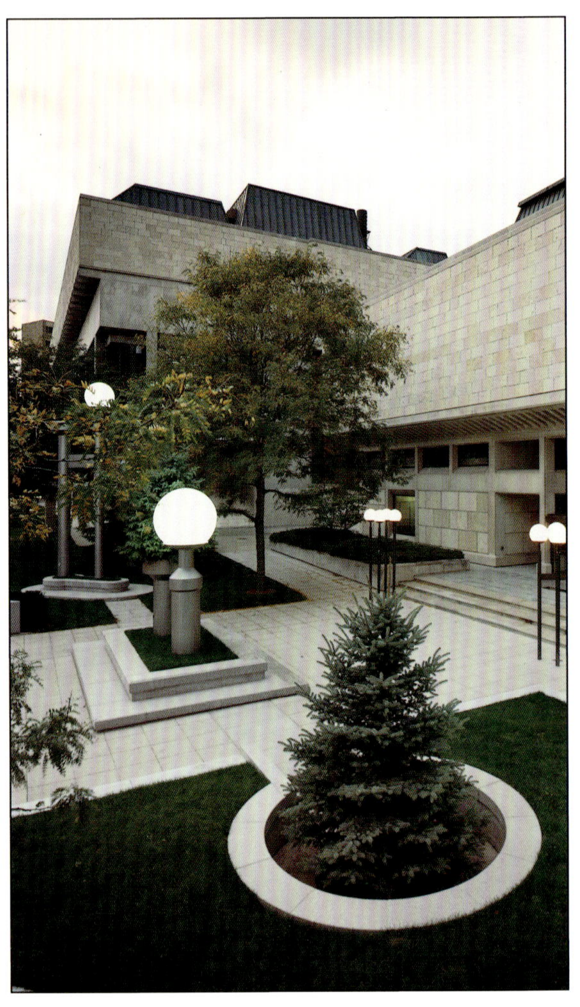

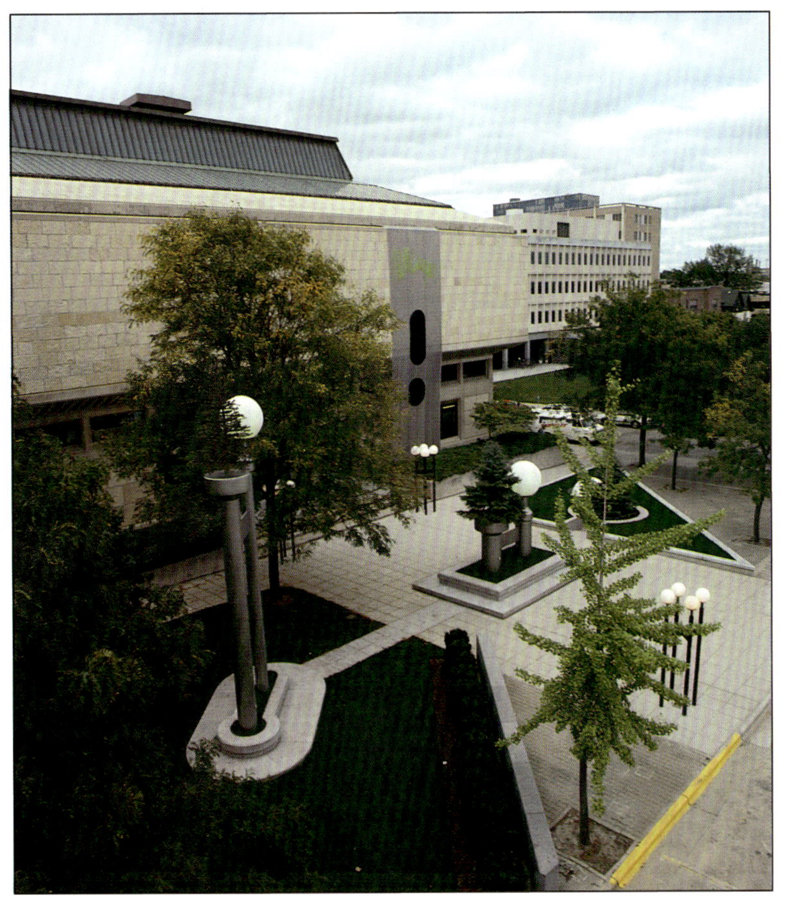

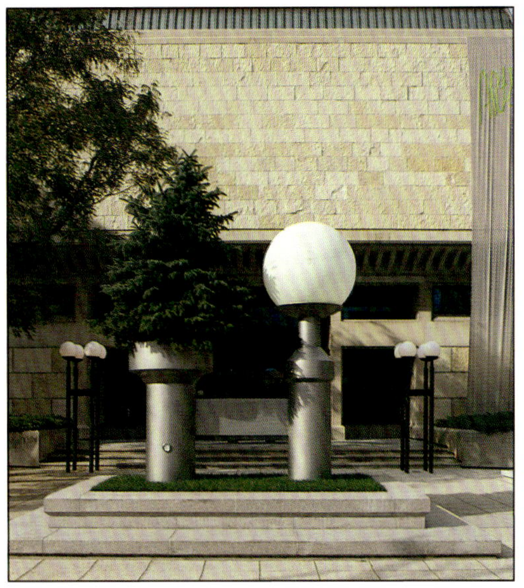

GENERATIONS

Commissioned by Elvehjem Museum of Art, 1990
Inaugurated September 14, 1991

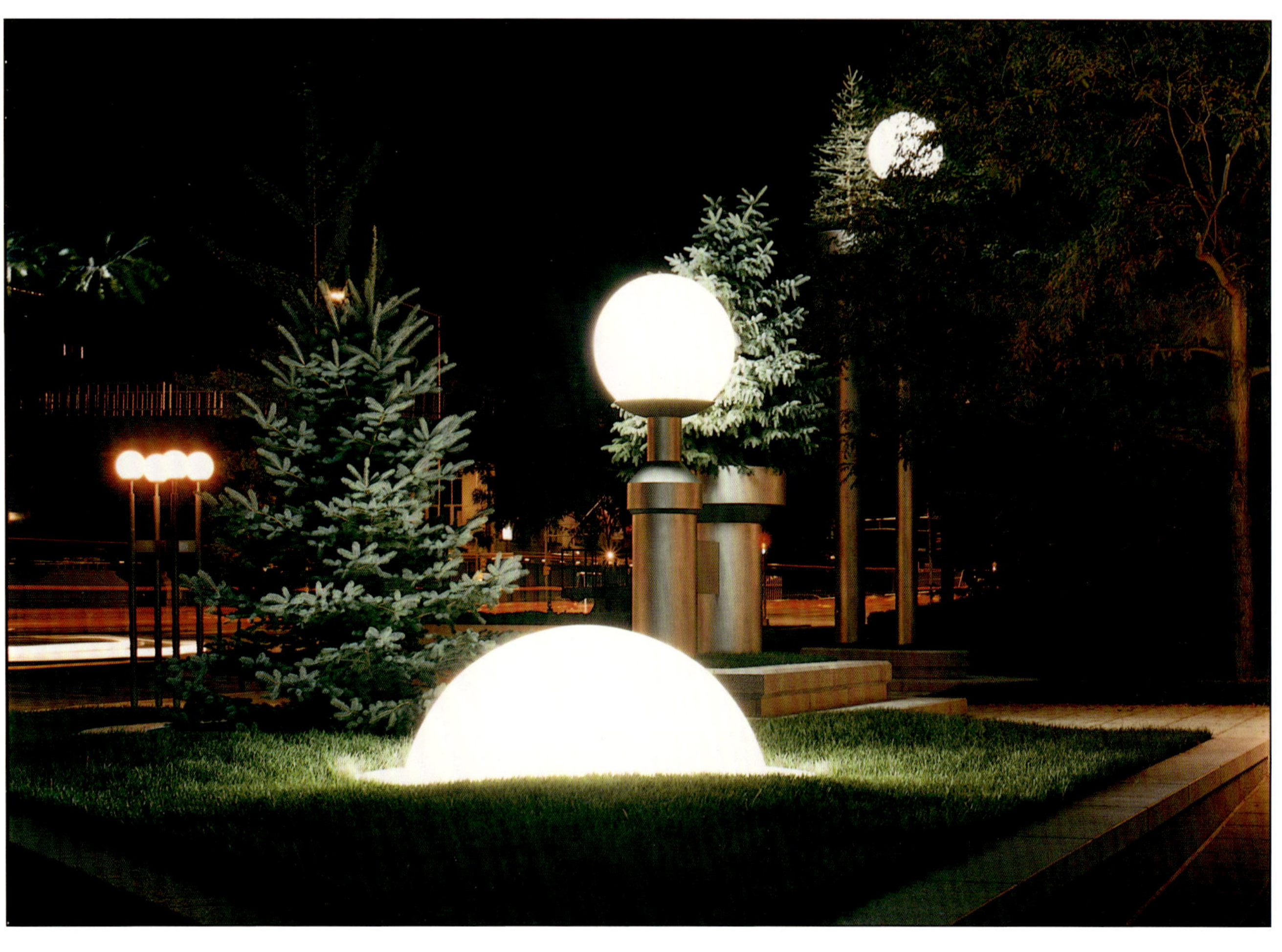

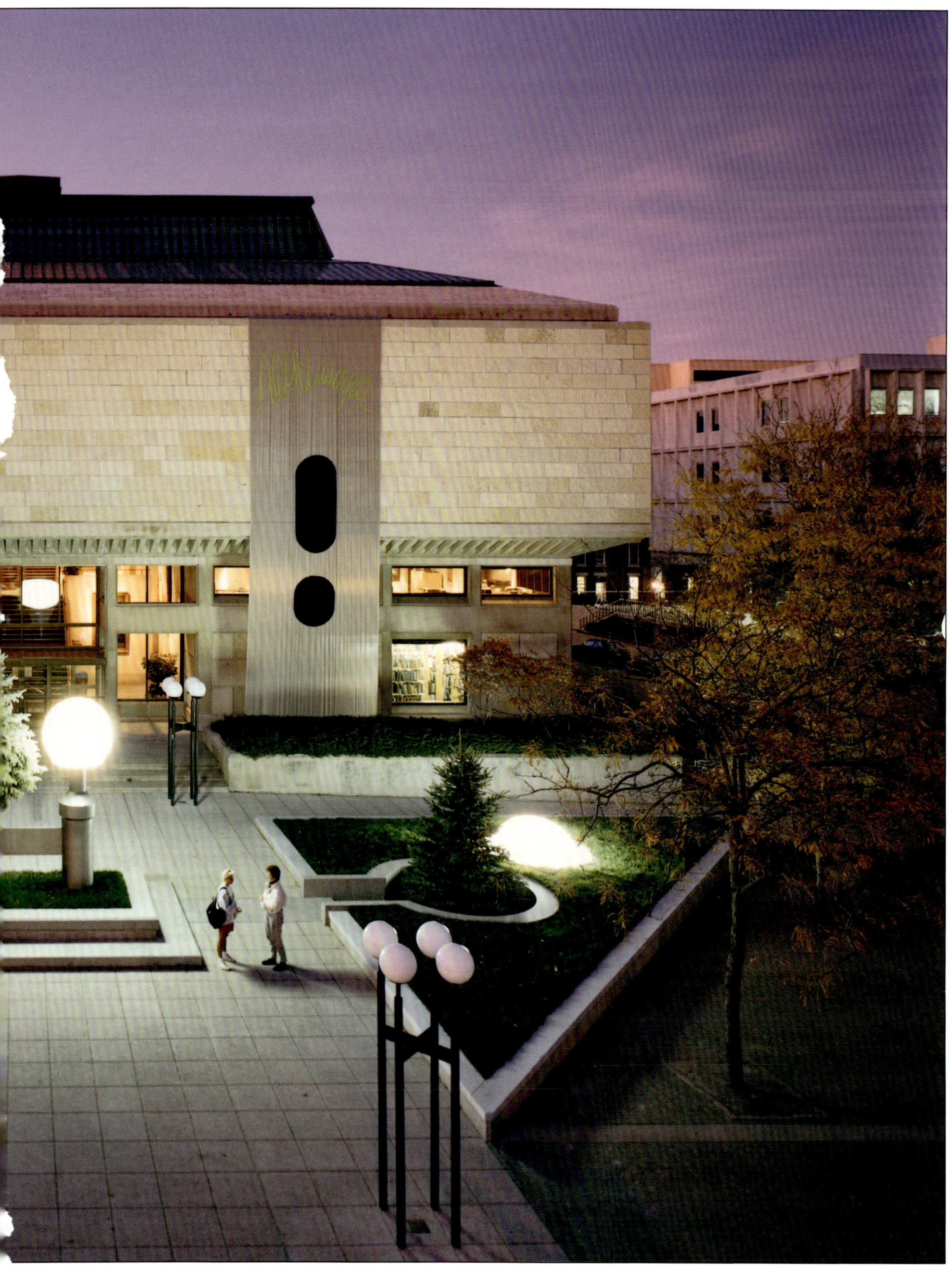

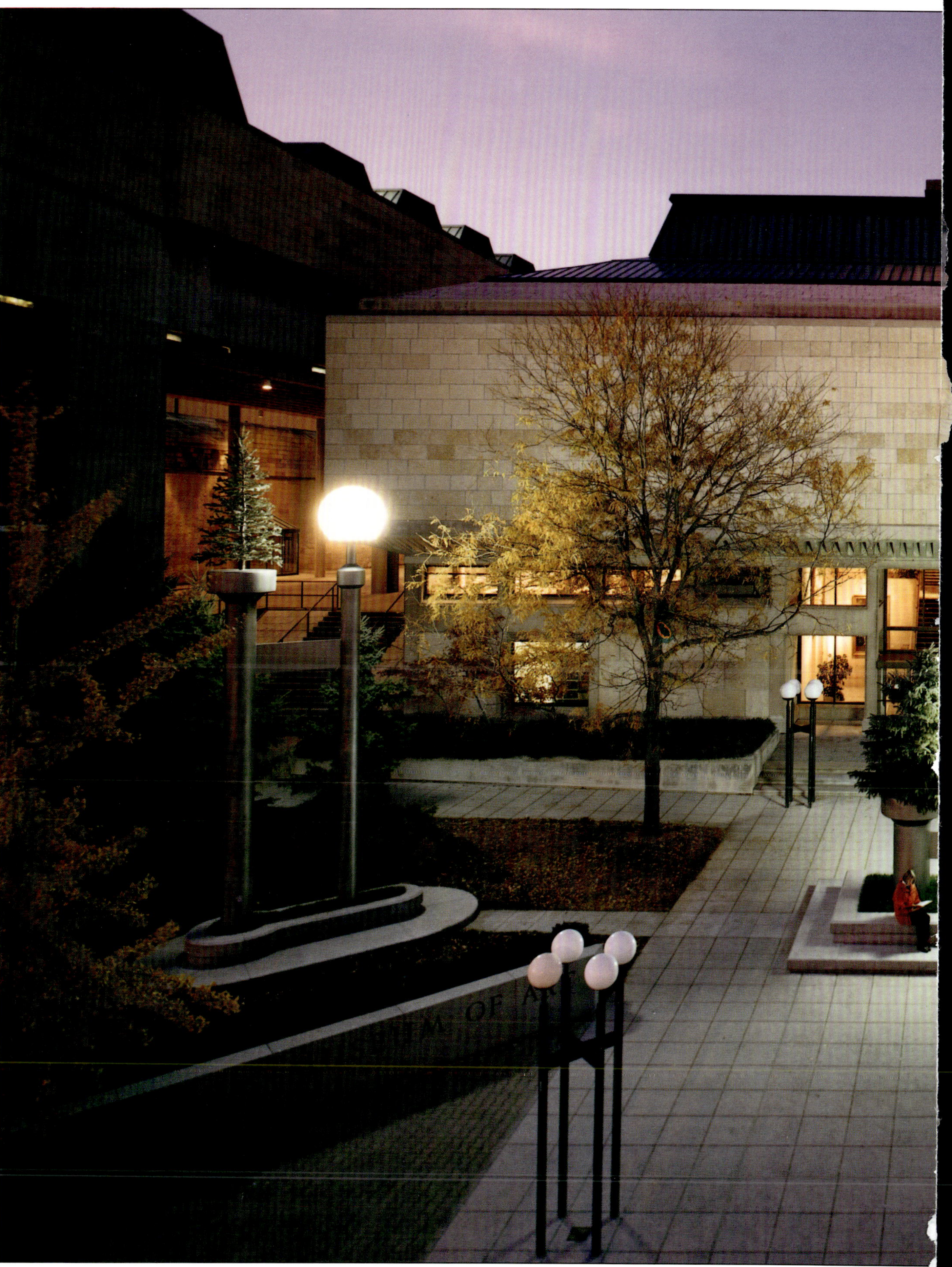

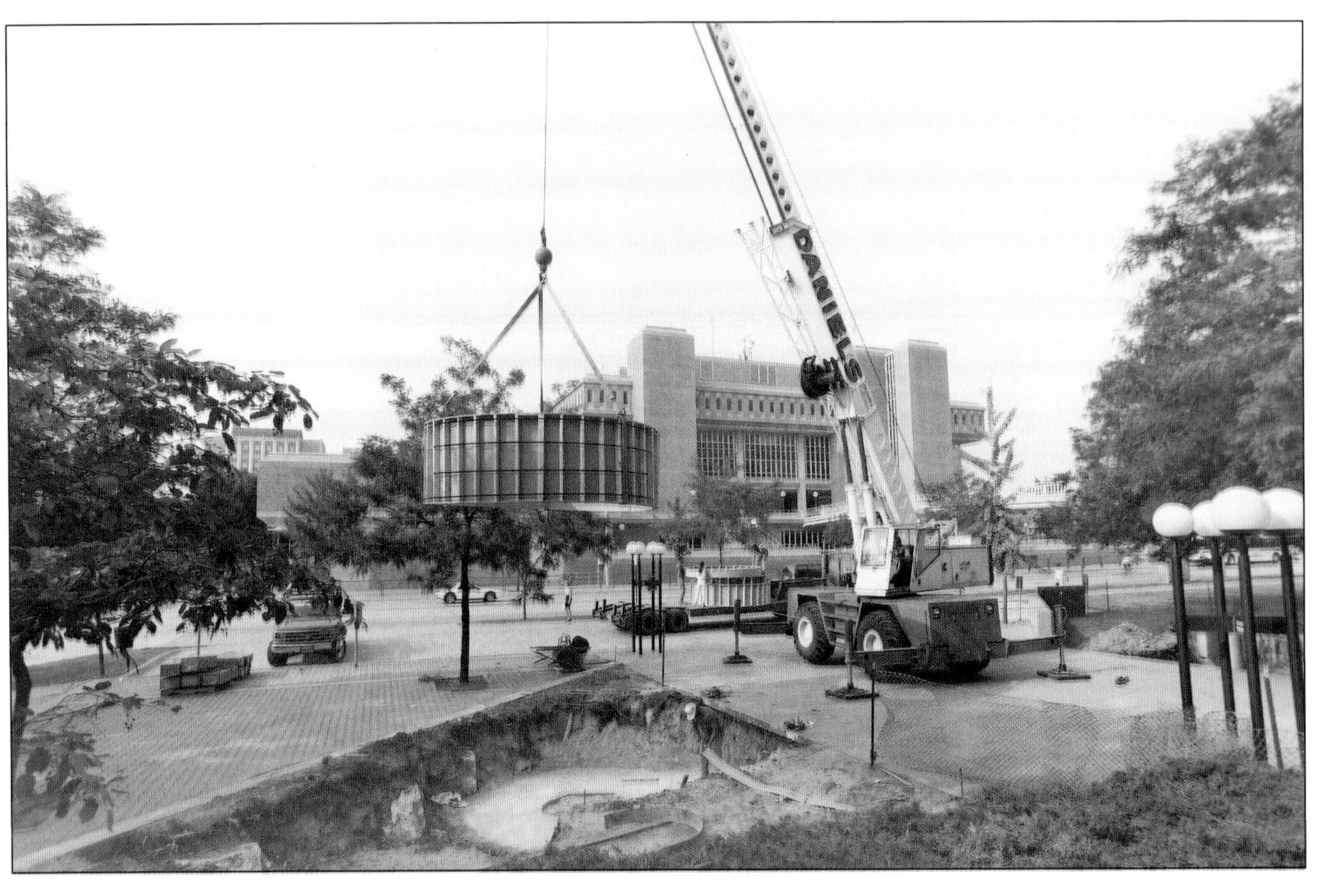

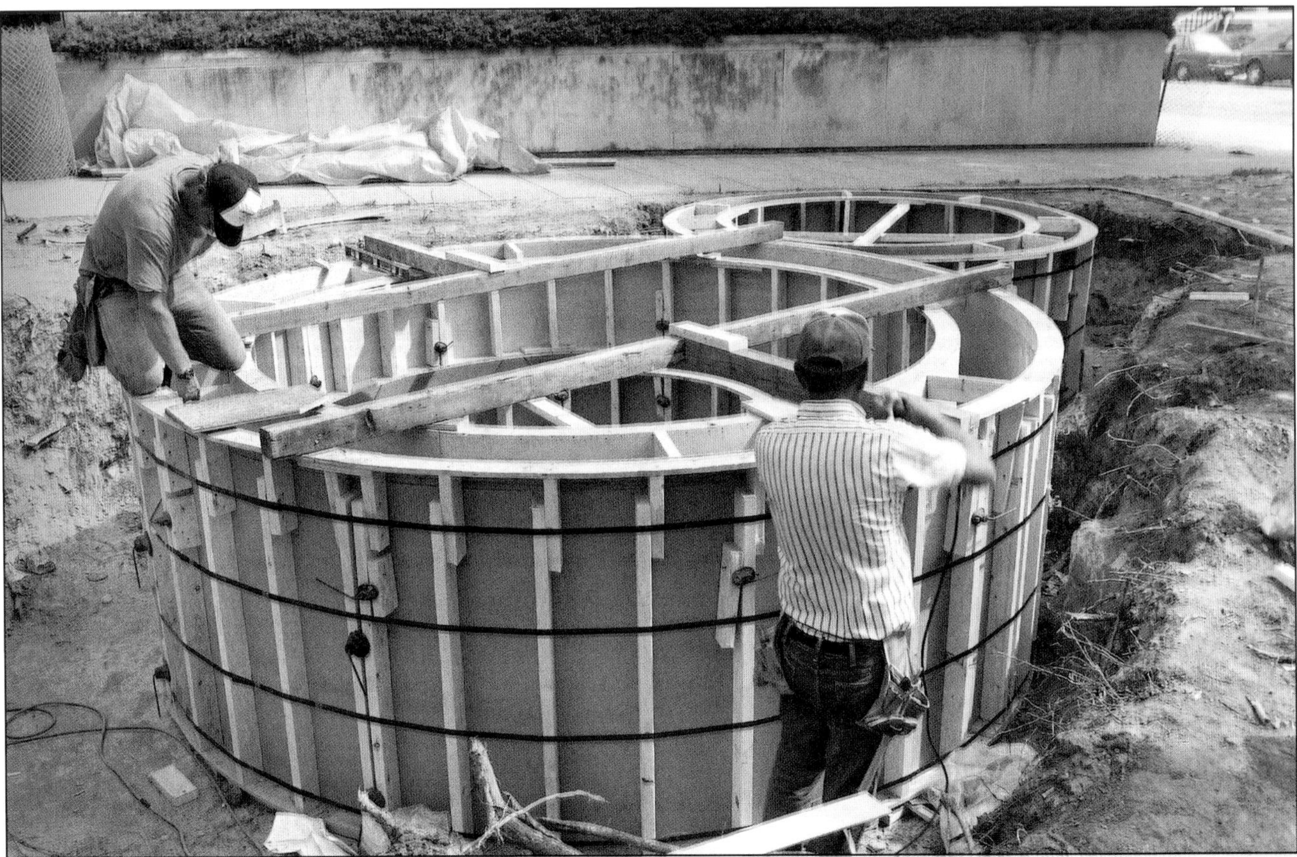

ABOVE: Placing the basic wood and cardboard form for the concrete footing of the sculpture in the east section
BELOW: Completing assemblage of form in east section after its height was extended by three inches

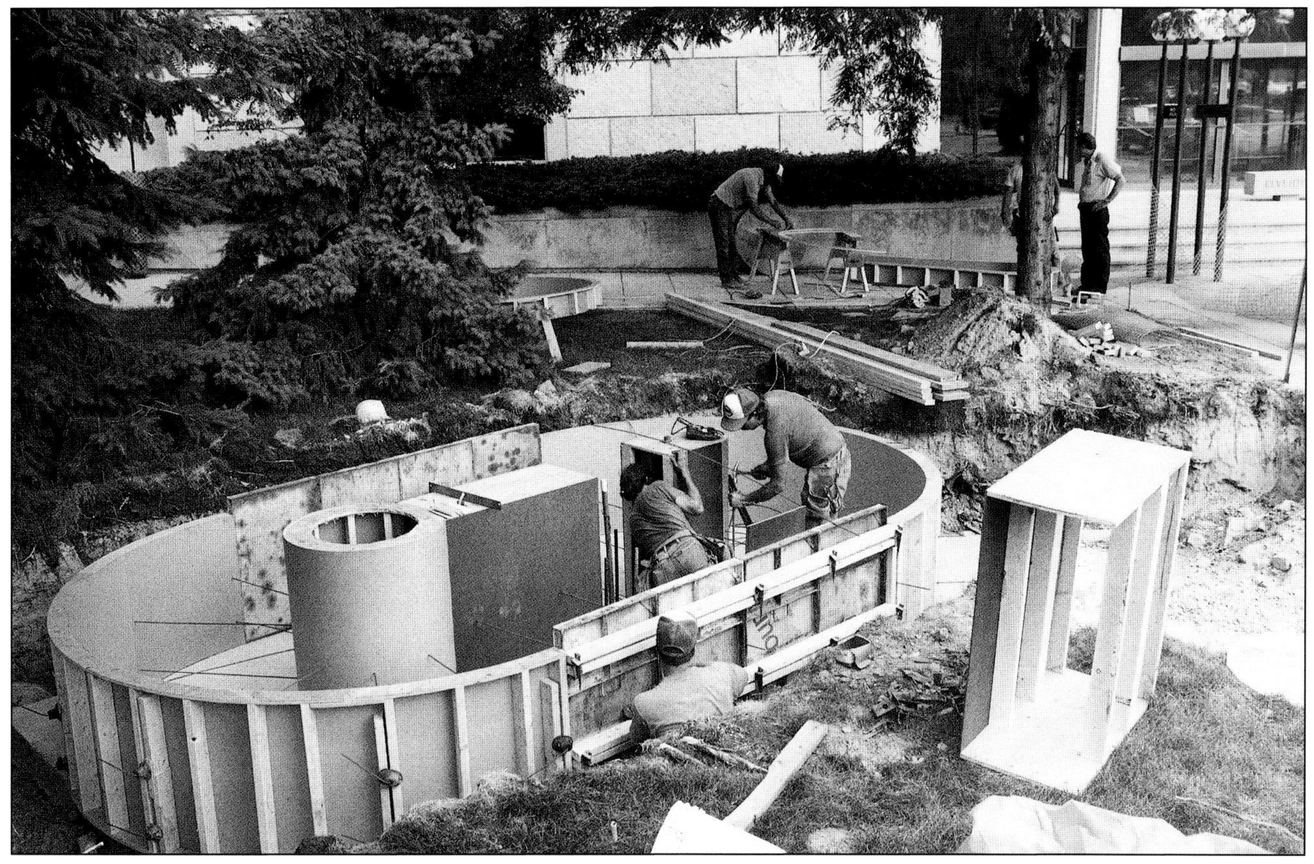

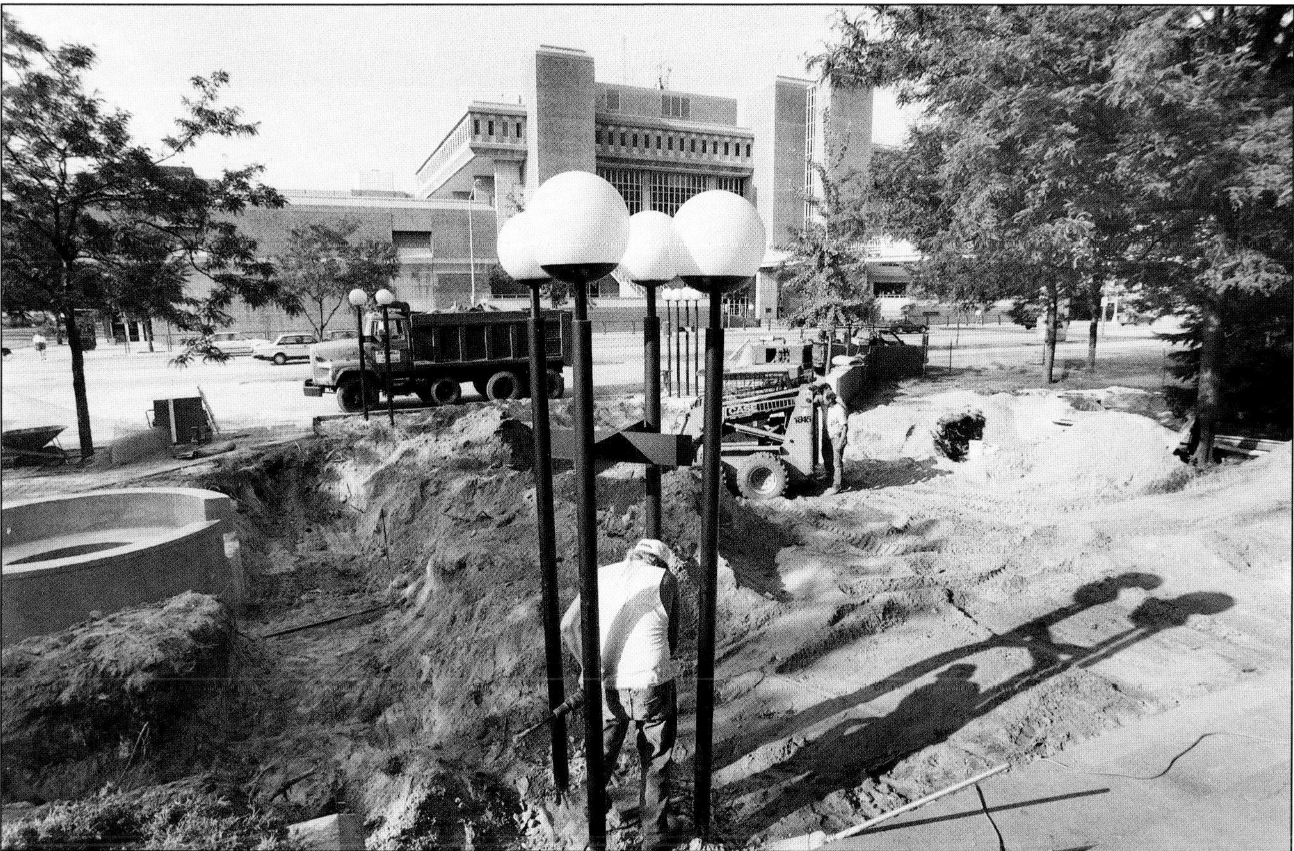

ABOVE: Assembling the form for the blp-shaped base in the east section
BELOW: Demolishing the central pavement once concrete footing in left and right sections were complete

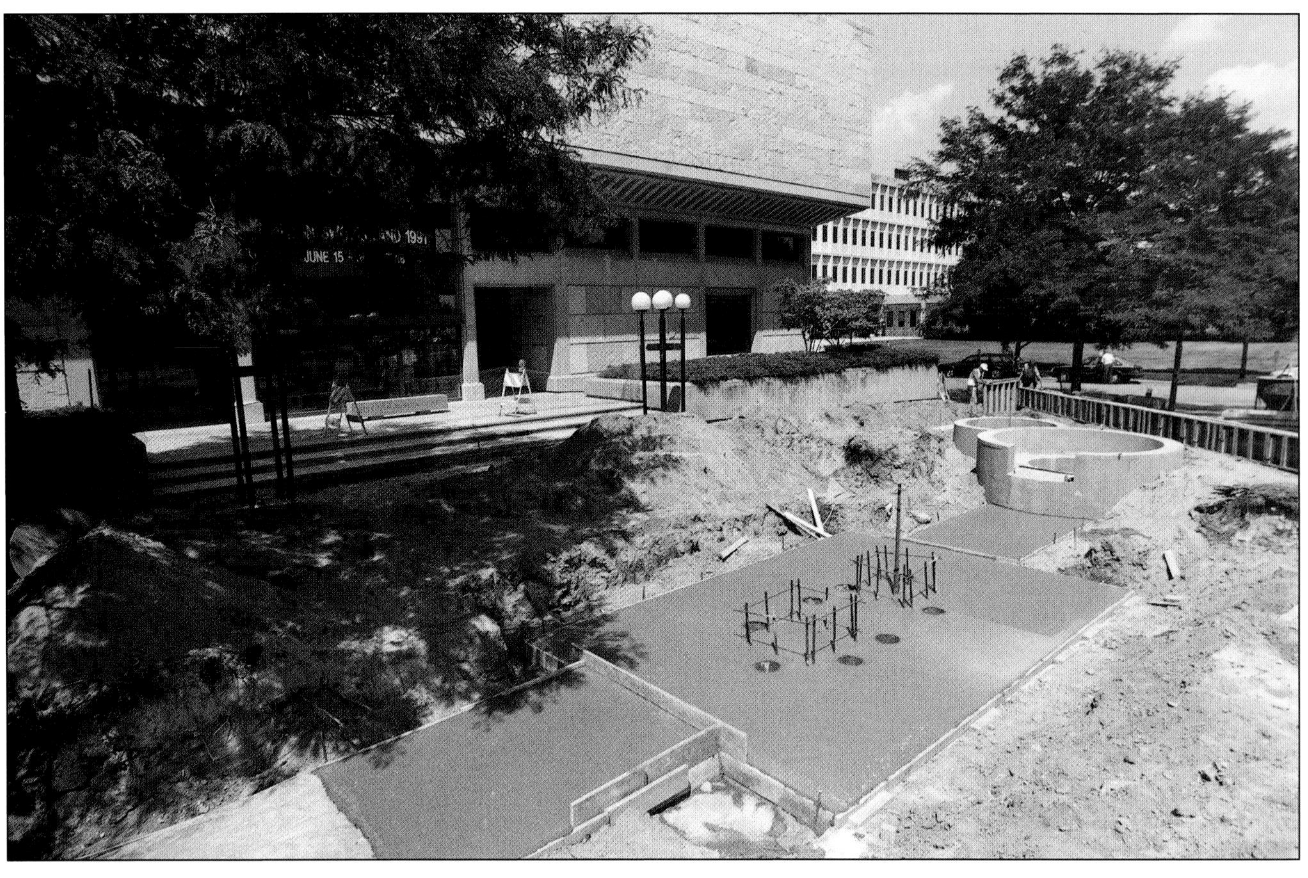

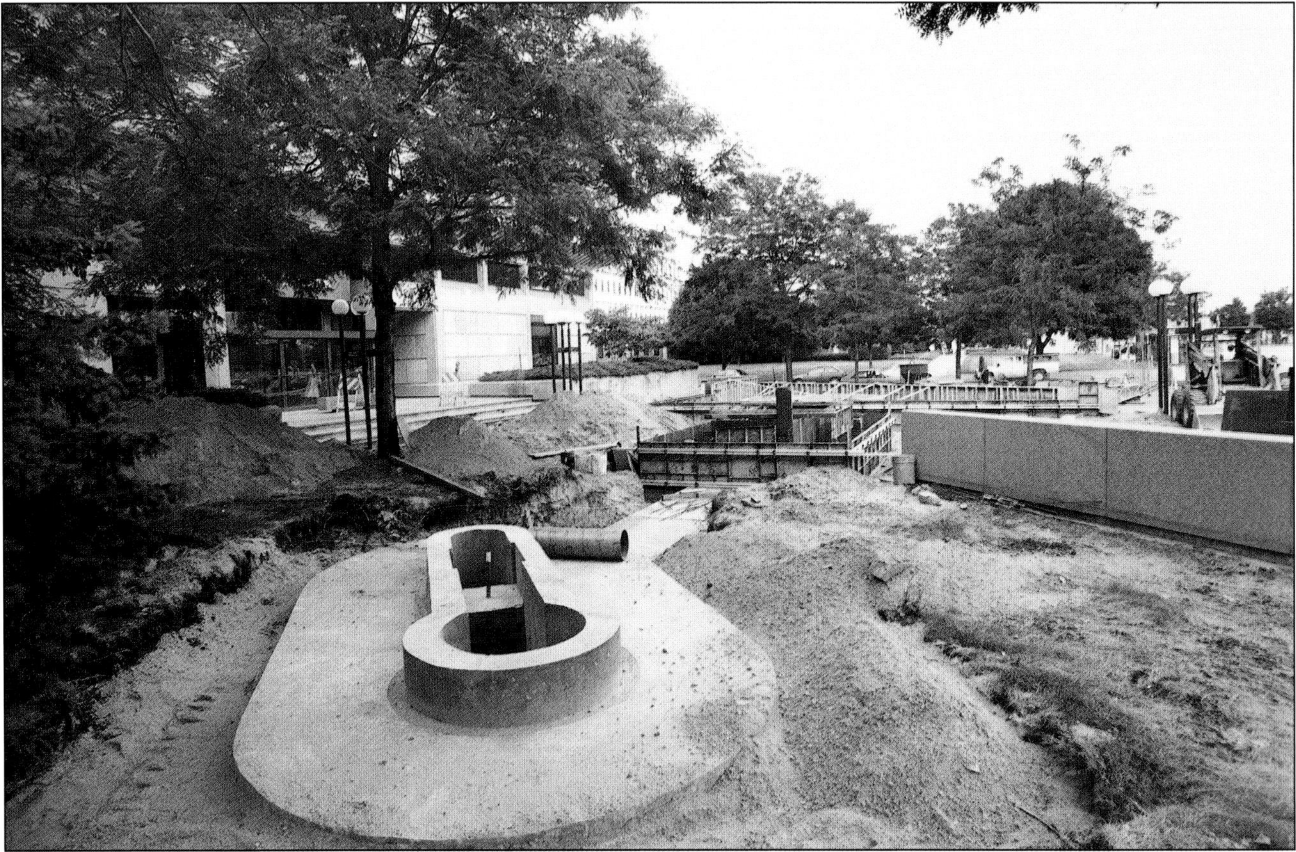

ABOVE: Preparing a level base for the footings in the central section
BELOW: Overview of the footings from west to east, with the blp-shaped base in the foreground

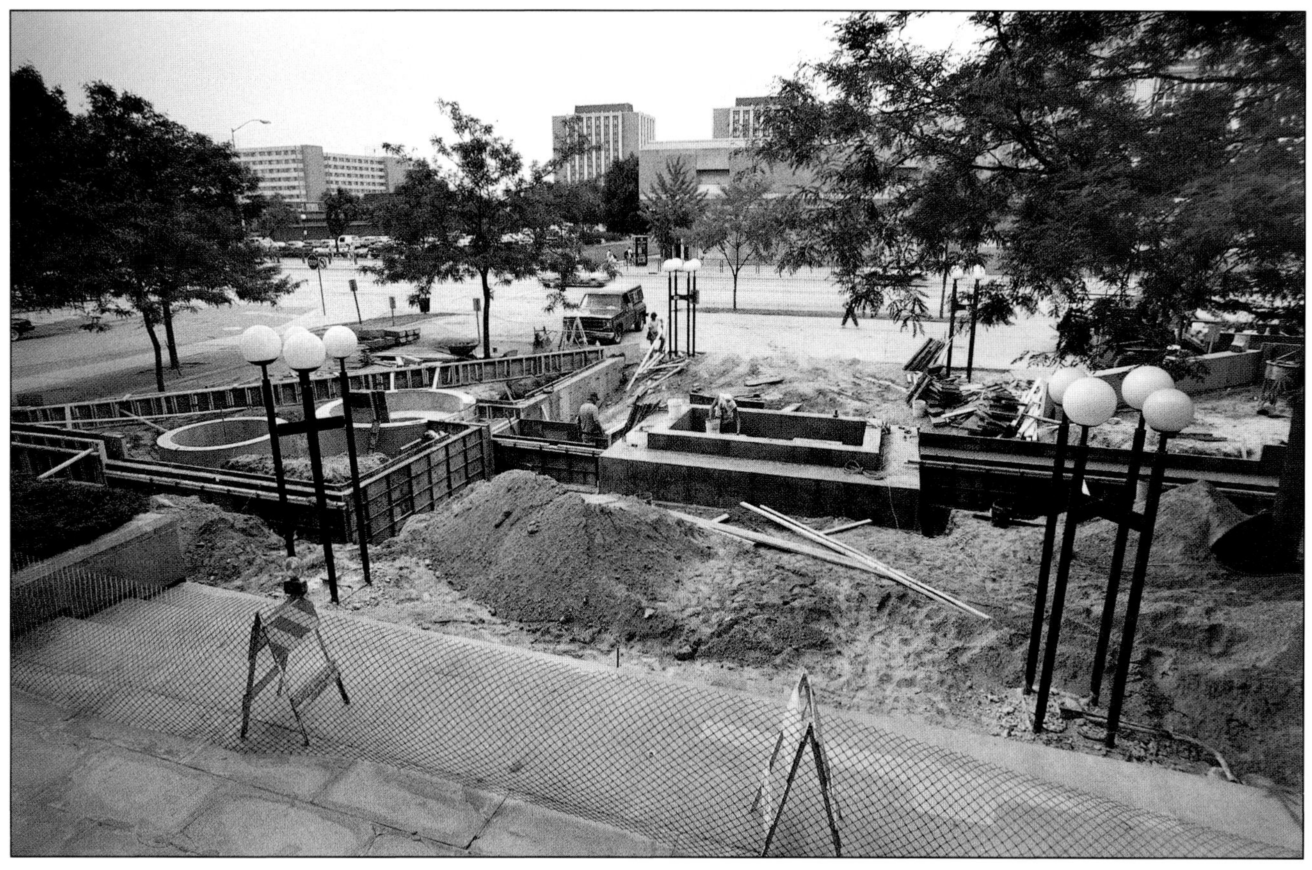

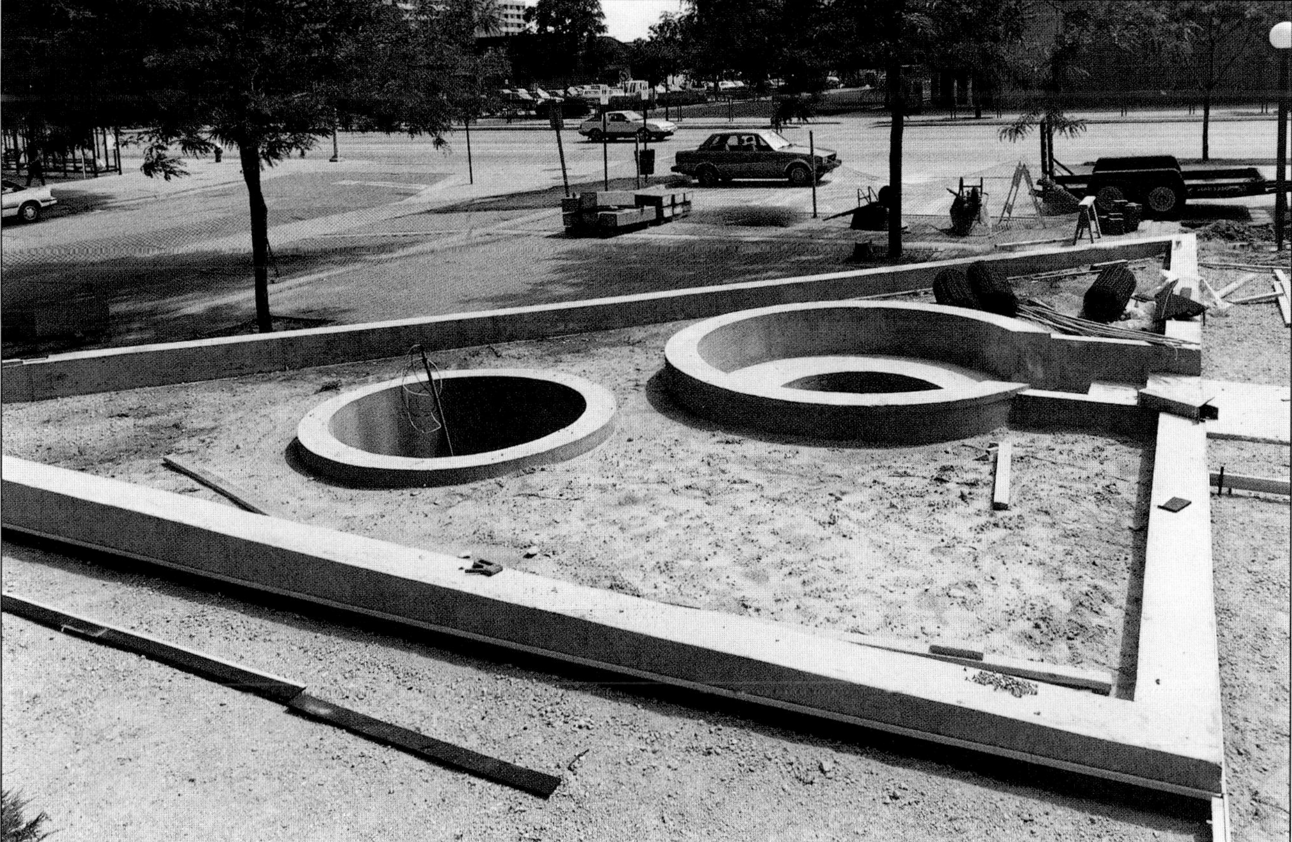

ABOVE: Assembling the forms for the concrete triangle shape in the east section
BELOW: The completed concrete footings for the east section

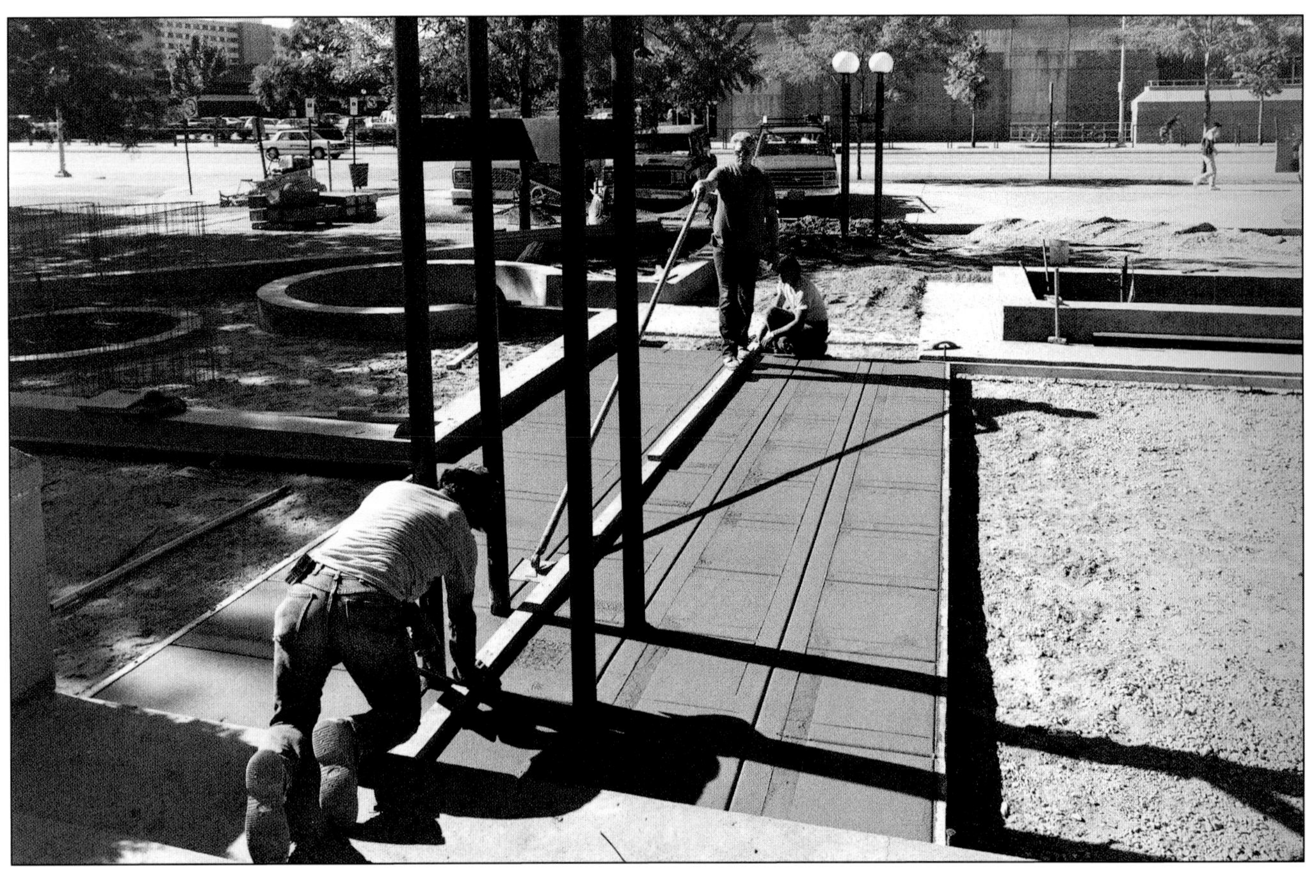

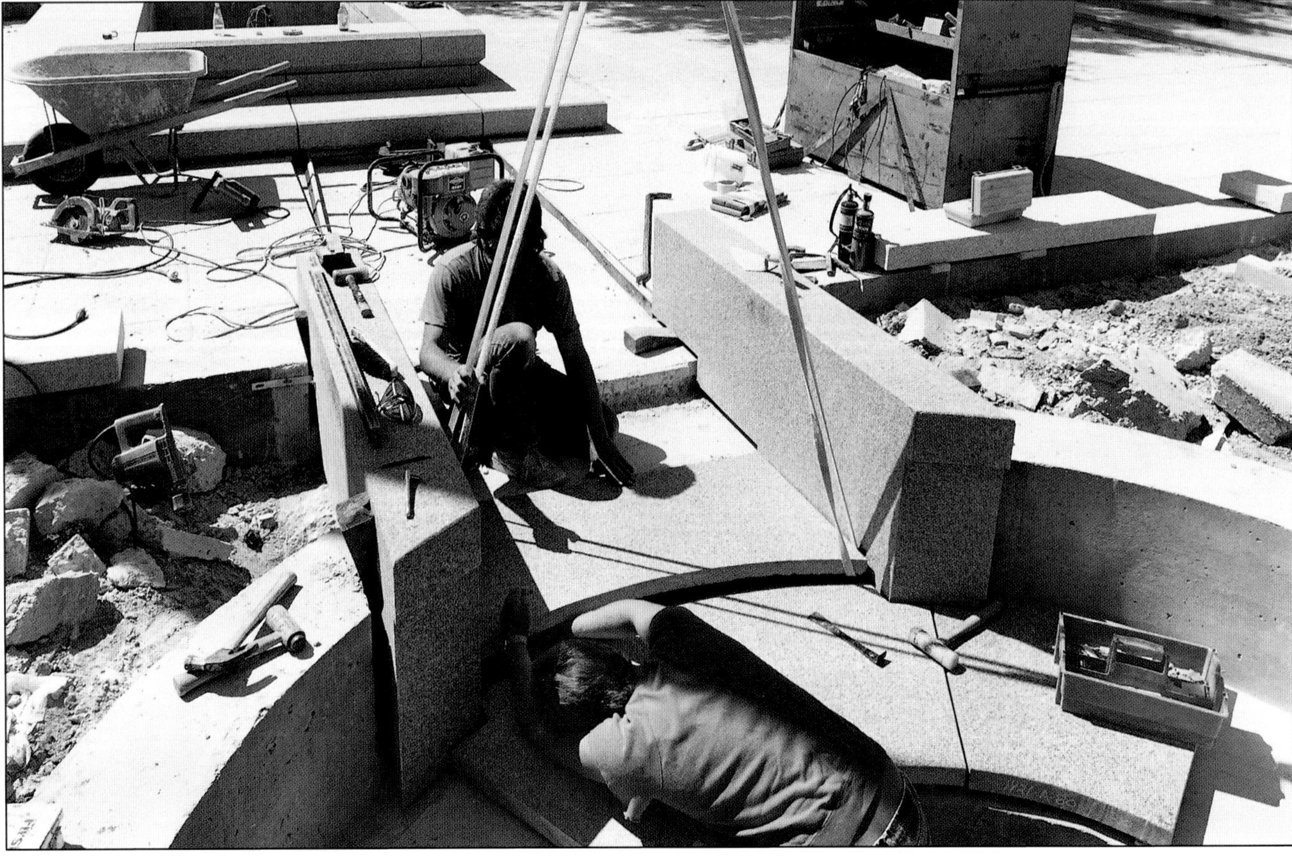

ABOVE: Workmen pouring and scoring the concrete for the central walkway
BELOW: Installing granite on top of the concrete base in the east section

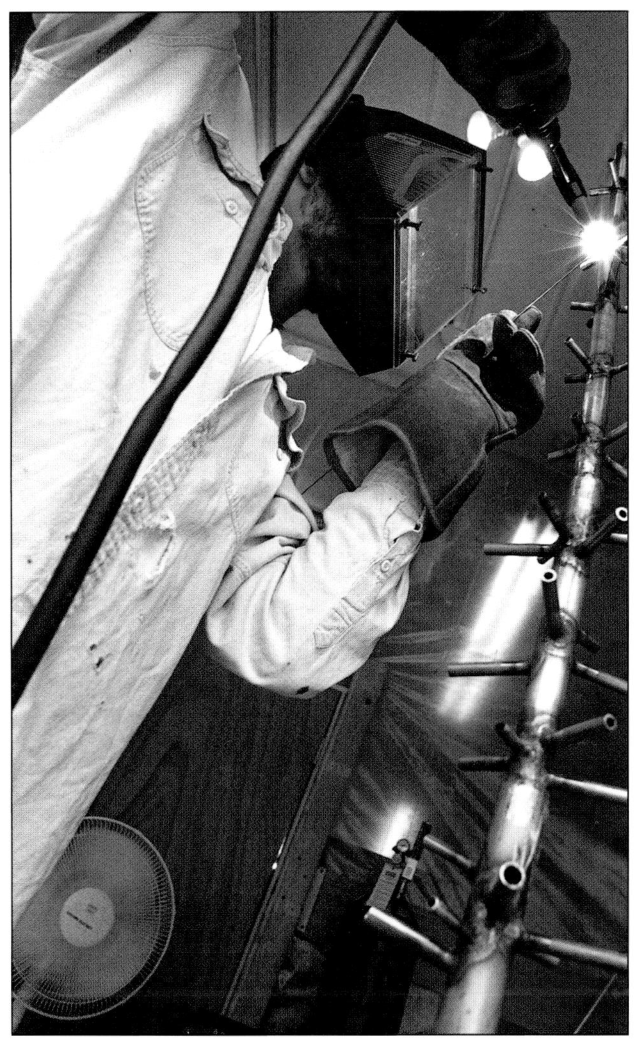

Fabricating the artificial tree in the artist's studio in Brooklyn, New York

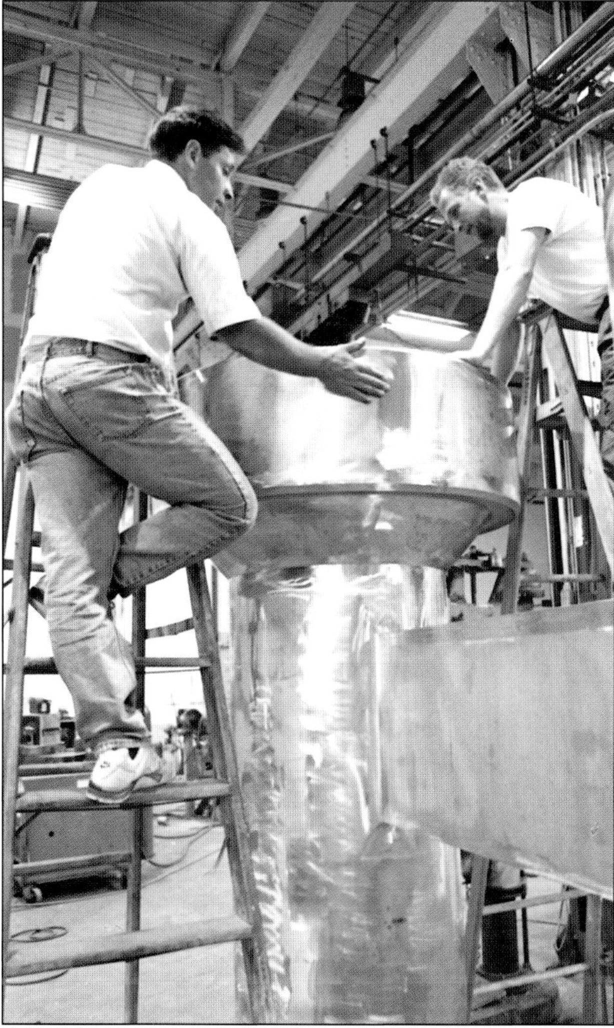

Tom MacGregor inspecting the steel columns being constructed

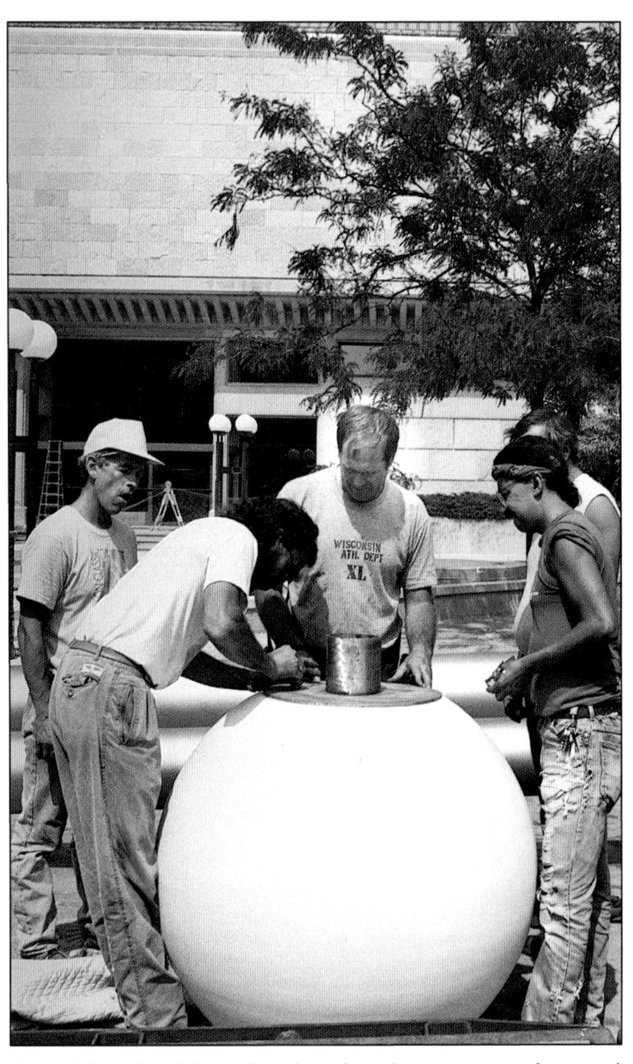

Assembling the globe to be placed on the twenty-two foot steel column

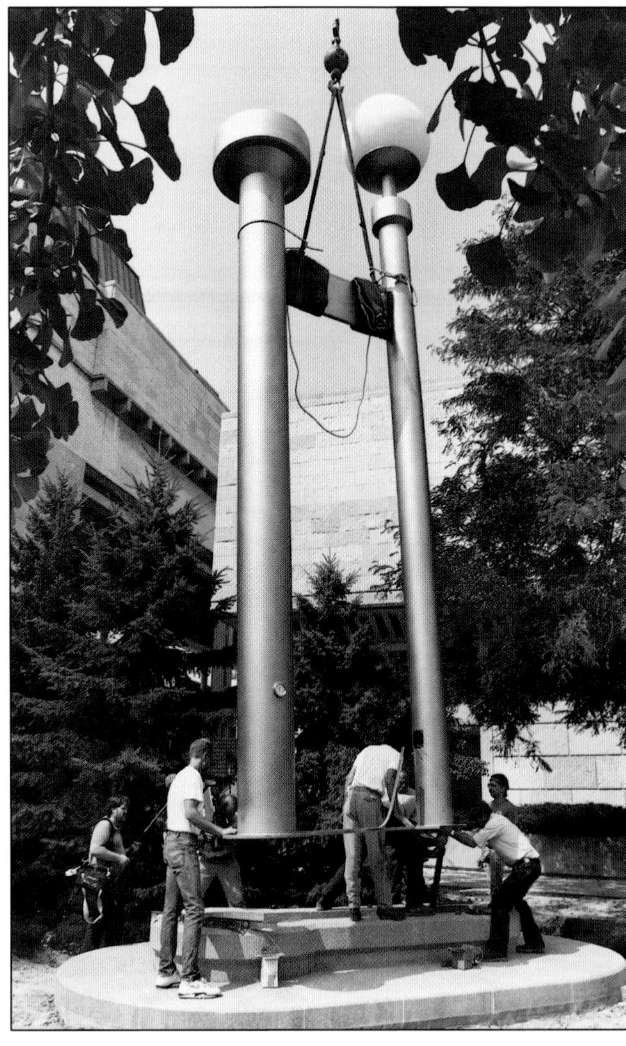

Installing the steel columns in the west and highest section

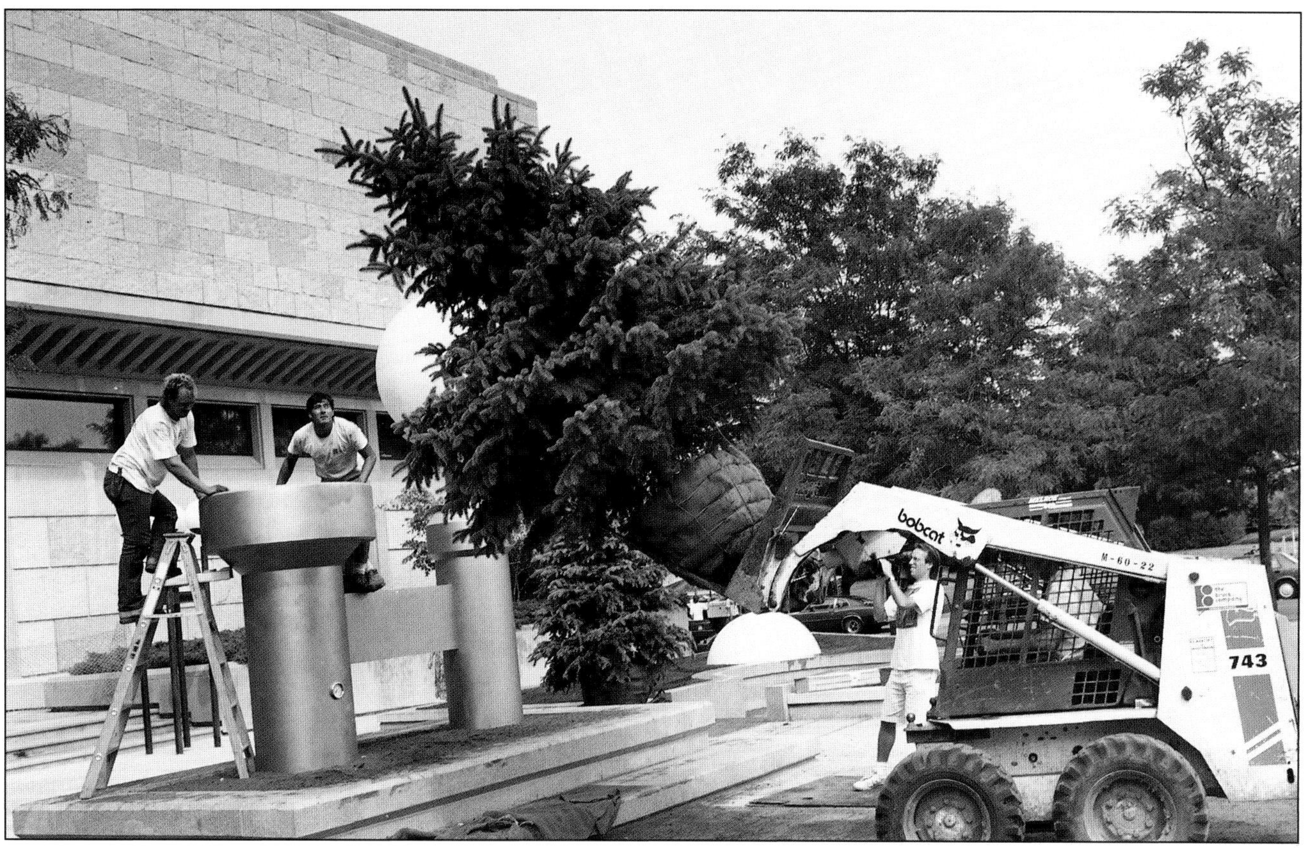

Hoisting into place the blue Colorado spruce in the central section

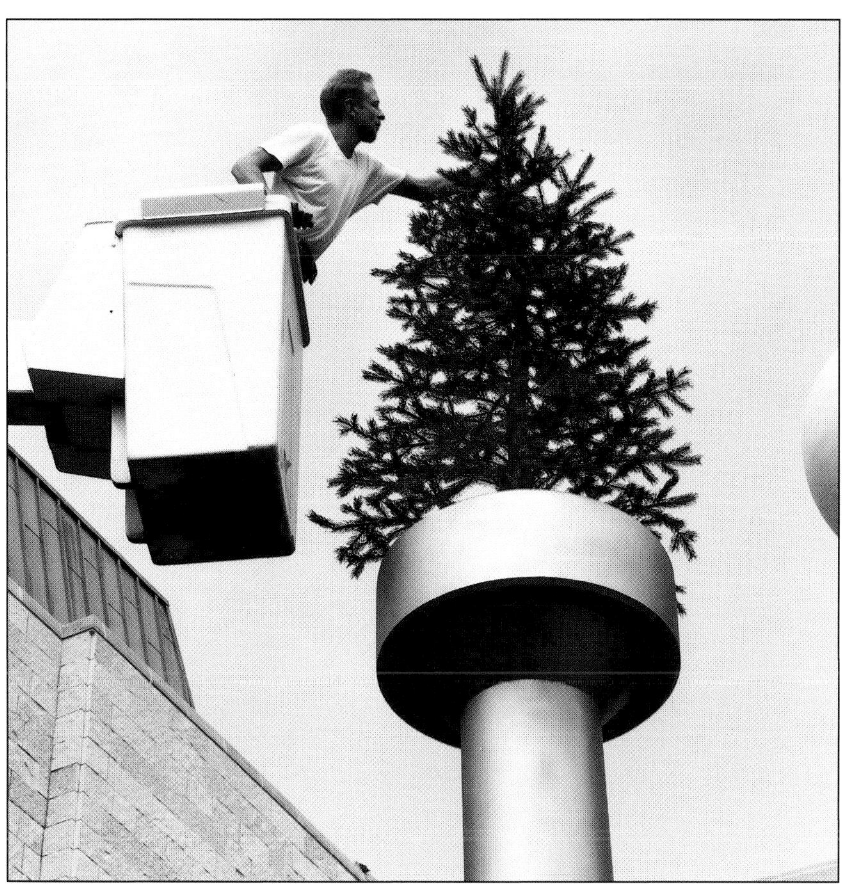

Installing the artificial tree during the topping-off ceremony at noon September 13, 1991

GENERATIONS:
A NEW WORK BY RICHARD ARTSCHWAGER

The Elvehjem Museum of Art, with its collection of over 14,000 objects and varied program of temporary exhibitions, is a unique resource and important cultural center for the academic community and for the citizens of Madison and Wisconsin. The museum, in a city with a population of only 175,000, has up to 120,000 visitors per year. However, despite its exceptional attendance and central location in the city, an audience study conducted by the museum staff in 1985 indicated that many incoming students, visitors to the city, as well as a surprising number of Madison residents remained unaware of the Elvehjem's presence. One of the reasons given for this lower-than-expected public profile was that there was nothing at the main entrance to call attention to the museum's presence or its unique function. The building, notwithstanding its strong public role and fine design, was not readily distinguishable from the surrounding university buildings.

As a consequence of the audience study, the museum staff, later that same year, developed a long-range plan, which included a recommendation calling for a large scale, preferably site-specific sculpture to be located on the building grounds in front of the Elvehjem's south facade facing onto busy University Avenue. The purpose of the proposed sculpture was to signal the unique function of the Elvehjem, to serve as a readily identifiable symbol of the museum, and generally to heighten awareness of the arts on campus. A memorandum in 1986 from the author to the UW Foundation explored the possibility of funding through a class anniversary gift such a project with the following conceptual parameters:

> '' . . . to purchase or to commission a large-scale work of art that can be located either in front of the building or directly on its south facade. The art work would have to be of a type and scale that would assure it visual prominence. It would have to be a strong work by a significant artist, a work capable of pointing up the teaching function of the museum. It must also be an appropriate addition to the Elvehjem's collections and an artwork of which the whole community can be proud. It is estimated that such a work and its installation will cost between $60,000 and $100,000.''

Nothing came of the initial exploration for funding, and the outdoor sculpture proposal made no progress beyond the conceptual stage for the next three years. In the spring of 1989 two unforeseen circumstances reactivated the search in earnest. E. David Cronon, dean of the College of Letters and Science, advised the author that the UW–Madison's Anonymous Fund Committee, of which he was then chairman, would seriously consider underwriting the project. At approximately the same time, Howard Hirsch, a Chicago collector, approached the author with a proposal ''to do something with outdoor sculpture on his farm in Hillsboro, Wisconsin, that would be interesting and in some way beneficial to the university.'' The confluence between the indeterminate nature of Mr. Hirsch's interests and the now real challenge of identifying an outdoor sculpture for the Elvehjem site lent itself to a common solution. The author suggested to Mr. Hirsch that a group of experts be invited to Madison to give an overview on recent developments in outdoor public art and to advise on the two specific ventures. Mr. Hirsch not only agreed but very generously funded the resulting symposium which was held on April 12, 1989.

SELECTION PROCESS

The five specialists who participated in the that program were Mary Beebe, director of the Stuart Collection of Outdoor Sculpture at the University of San Diego; Jennifer Dowley, director of the Headlands Project in Sausalito, California; Patricia Fuller, independent curator and former director of the Art in Public Places Program at the National Endowment for the Arts; David Furchgott, executive director of the International Sculpture Center located in Washington, D.C.; and Cesar Trasobares, director of the Metro Dade Art in Public Places Program in Miami, Florida. Following their general presentation, which was open to students, faculty, and interested members of the public, they met first with Mr. Hirsch and then with the five members of the museum's regularly appointed Accessions Committee which reviews and sanctions all additions to the museum's permanent collection. The latter committee consisted of Barbara Buenger and Frank Horlbeck, professors in the Department of Art History; Patricia K. Mansfield, professor of textiles and design in the Department of Family Resources and Consumer Science; Wayne Taylor, artist and professor in the Department of Art; and the author who as museum director served as the committee chairman.

Together the two groups reviewed the Elvehjem's collection policies and educational mission, inspected the designated site between the building and University Avenue, discussed the museum's rationale for placing a large-scale sculpture in front of the building, and advised on procedures for its selection. The wide-ranging knowledge and cumulative experience of the five visiting specialists were crucial to the initial stages of the project, for they helped to shape the method and direction of the Elvehjem's search and made the members of the Elvehjem Accessions Committee more sensitive to current issues in public art, as well as to the concerns of artists. However, at the same time, the visiting committee very carefully refrained from imposing their individual aesthetic judgments. They made it clear that if the search was ultimately to be successful, it would have to be directed by an Elvehjem committee.

The visiting panelists reaffirmed the Accession Committee's preexisting inclination to commission a new work of art rather than to purchase an existing one. The Accessions Committee had given some thought to the latter possibility based on the premise that such an approach would eliminate the element of risk: judging the quality and suitability of an existing sculpture for the site would be far easier than successfully projecting a maquette or a concept-drawing onto an abstract site plan. An existing sculpture would have also had the advantage of reassuring potential underwriters, especially important in Madison where public art commissions had been controversial in recent years. Ultimately, however, the Accessions Committee came to a consensus that a commission was preferable since it would be consonant with the recent collecting policy of the Elvehjem and its aspirations to leadership in the visual arts.

The experience of the five visiting experts established that a work of the scale and quality desired by the museum would cost significantly more than the $100,000 which we originally projected. Thus immediately following the departure of the panelists, the museum readjusted its budget for the planned sculpture to a more realistic $250,000 and, based on this figure, submitted a grant request for an unspecified amount to the Anonymous Fund Committee. One month later, the Anonymous Fund Committee awarded the Elvehjem $100,000 toward the project. The difference between this amount and the new projected total was to be made up with the earnings from the museum's art purchase endowment, since the proposed sculpture was to be added to the museum's permanent collection, different from other acquisitions only in scale and placement outdoors.

In 1985, when the author first advanced the idea to the Accessions Committee of adding a large-scale outdoor sculpture to the museum's permanent collection, there was little discussion about the actual selection process. However, with the funding for the project in place, this committee, whose express office it is to review and sanction all art proposed for acquisition by museum staff, was appropriately charged with the responsibility for the new piece: its veteran members were familiar with the museum's collecting policies and directions, while, at the same time, based on their previous service, the museum was comfortable with their ability to judge the quality and artistic merits of contemporary sculpture. However, given the unique permanent and public nature of the proposed acquisition, the author invited Donald Crawford, dean of the College of Letters and Science, Horst Lobe, senior architect of the UW's Department of Planning and Construction, and Jane Coleman, a community leader and member of the Elvehjem Council to join the regular Accessions Committee in the search for the new sculpture. Each of these individuals had something special to contribute to the project: Don Crawford, a philosopher whose interest was aesthetics, replaced David Cronon as dean of the College of Letters and Science in July of 1989 and was in a position to guide the placement of the sculpture through the complex administrative processes of the university; Horst Lobe, who also had the advantage of having served on several public art search committees in the community, could advise the museum on practical issues related to contracts and construction; Jane Coleman would be an excellent indicator of community opinion and an advocate for the new work.

Even before the visit of the five specialists discussed above, the original Accessions Committee had abandoned the notion of an open competition in favor of a limited one, which seemed more manageable from the logistical standpoint and would be more attractive to well-established artists. Such an approach would also give the museum greater control over the final outcome. With this in mind, the Accessions Committee had specifically requested the five visiting experts to develop a list of artists for its further consideration who, in their opinion, would be particularly sympathetic to what the museum wished to achieve with its outdoor sculpture. The other chief criterion was that the artists be accomplished, not necessarily well known, but that they be recognized by curators and critics for their contributions to developments in the contemporary visual arts. However, at the same time, it was not imperative that their achievements be in large-scale outdoor work. The latter could be an area into which they had recently ventured but for which they had demonstrated an unequivocal interest. The Accessions Committee felt strongly that the Elvehjem commission was to represent an opportunity for the artist as well as to be a major addition to the collection.

The newly constituted ad hoc sculpture committee readily espoused the concept of an invitational approach to the selection process. And, once the visiting experts had done their work, the next logical step was to invite each of the ten recommended artists to submit a model for the committee's consideration. However, as the committee studied the logistics, as well as the ethics, of such an approach, it found that even such a limited competition was highly problematic. One of the key considerations in the decision to abandon the competitive approach was the fact that the visual arts community, in general, finds competitions distasteful, each artist preferring his or her work to be judged on its own merits. An invitational competition was still a competition. Also, for a university or a museum to engage in such a tactic would demonstrate insensitivity to concerns of artists, and this in itself had the high probability of precluding the best artists from participating. This view was corroborated in a telephone conversation between the author and one well-known artist who refused even to discuss the project if the Elvehjem was simultaneously considering any one else.

The financial implications of an invitational competition also proved prohibitive. The members of the Anonymous Fund Committee which, as a condition of its grant, had recommended that the sculpture selection be carried out by a competition, had not foreseen travel expenses and remuneration to the artists for their submissions. In the sculpture committee's deliberations about this issue, it became clear that in order for an artist to submit a site-specific model, he or she would have to come to Madison to view the site at least once and return with the model for its presentation and explication to the committee. There was also the question of paying the artists for their concepts as well as reimbursing them for the materials required to build the models. Expecting artists to produce site-specific models or drawings simply in the hopes of getting a commission was not only perceived by artists and the sculpture committee as exploitative and unethical, but it also conflicted with the guidelines set down by the arts community as well as the National Endowment for the Arts. Published guidelines recommend that artists be paid up to ten percent of the total budget for their work on a project. The committee concluded that the costs of a competition involving ten artists, which adhered to recommended principles, would deplete the funds available for the sculpture itself or would require raising additional monies. The committee rejected the first option since the funds designated for the project were already at the low end of what a sculpture of the quality and magnitude appropriate to the Elvehjem site normally cost. Fund-raising was equally unacceptable given the weak economic forecasts

and the fact that the university was already engaged in a major capital campaign.

The sculpture committee finally decided that instead of a competition based on the comparison of submitted models, it would review the existing work of each of the ten recommended artists and invite one of them to submit a model. Should this work prove unsatisfactory for any reason, the commission could either select one of the remaining nine and so forth down the list, or seek additional recommendations. However, the latitude and flexibility built into this process proved completely unnecessary as the committee was ultimately unanimous in support of the model submitted by its first-choice artist. Although it would be decidedly unethical to name the ten individuals whom the visiting panelists advocated since most of them remain unaware of their candidacy, discrete mention of the sculpture committee's deliberations about their work will elucidate the process which led to the selection of Richard Artschwager.

Unquestionably the work of all ten artists was of the highest aesthetic merit; the visiting experts had made a careful selection. However, in the course of its preliminary deliberations about outdoor sculpture, the sculpture committee had developed a set of criteria which came into play as the work of the ten recommended artists was reviewed. One artist's work which was predominantly environmental, involving mounds and earthworks, although intellectually fascinating lacked the vertical and distinctively monumental presence needed to distinguish the museum from its surroundings. Furthermore, such work seemed to offer a bulwark against a public that was already faced with a rather imposing and formidable architectural structure. The committee also eliminated artists whose work was predominantly horizontal in design and artists whose work was of a massive three-dimensional nature, approaches which would seem to impose barriers or visual obstacles between passersby on University Avenue and the Elvehjem building. Work that was narrative in nature either through the use of figurative imagery or language was considered to be too specific to have the timeless quality required of a permanent installation. The committee also dropped from consideration work which would require attachment to the building itself in order to avoid involving the State Building Commission in the selection process; the new work was to be an addition to the museum's collection and not a ''public project.'' Several practical concerns were also key factors in the selection process. Since museum staff had no prior experience in fabrication, installation, or budgeting of large scale outdoor work, the committee deemed it essential that the artist be able to demonstrate convincingly that the work could be realized and come within budget. Finally, since the Elvehjem's new work would have to withstand the dramatic shifts of the rigorous Wisconsin climate, the adaptability of each artist's work to durable materials was an important factor.

As part of the review process and just prior to the selection of Richard Artschwager, the Elvehjem's outdoor sculpture committee once again deliberated acquiring an existing work. Although this alternative had been discouraged by the five visiting experts, the new committee felt that its own search would be incomplete if this avenue was not explored. Also, and justifiably so, the reconsideration of this option was prompted by a certain amount of trepidation about the responsibility of commissioning a work of art that would, unlike other acquisitions, be permanently placed in front of the building and serve as a signature piece for the entire institution. However, after significant research, discussion, and even a site visit by one creator of a work under consideration, the committee concluded that purchasing an existing work for the Elvehjem site would be no less, and perhaps even more, difficult and unpredictable than a site-specific commission. Existing large-scale outdoor works generally proved elusive, difficult to identify, and difficult to trace. Slides of those that were considered proved to be as abstract as models or drawings. Adapting an existing work of art to the singular Elvehjem site also posed special creative challenges of its own which, the committee ultimately concluded, was better entrusted to an artist.

Returning to the work by the artists originally recommended for a commission by the visiting experts, the members of the Elvehjem committee were increasingly attracted by the direct impact and the strong physical presence of Richard Artschwager's sculpture. His interest in visual and physical space, in the relation between his work and its surroundings, and in the architectural implications of his work, all recommended him. His intellectual and aesthetic independence were also particularly appealing to a committee representing an academic community. Furthermore, Artschwager was already familiar with the university where he had been artist-in-residence in November of 1968. If there was a concern, it was that the committee could find little information about Artschwager's large-scale outdoor sculpture. This aspect of his work was little documented since Artschwager's first such piece, the untitled concrete tree in Münster, Germany, was only realized in 1987. Nonetheless, the committee's strong interest in the quality of Artschwager's work prevailed, and in April 1990 he was invited to come to Madison to view the

site and discuss the Elvehjem project. The meeting was mutually inspiring, and the committee invited the artist to submit a proposal.

ARTIST'S PROPOSALS

A conceptual model was completed and shipped to Madison several weeks later (fig. 1). At its unveiling on July 9, 1990 the committee's initial reaction consisted of stunned silence; the model did not correspond with anyone's immediate expectations. Although the committee had used the term site-specific in its original deliberations, in retrospect, it seems that what was understood by that term was "harmonious." Based on the original requirement that the sculpture have a distinctive monumental character so that it could serve as a signature piece for the museum, the committee had envisioned an autonomous vertical piece which in its design and color was aesthetically compatible with the architecture of the building and the arrangement of the existing plaza. This limited concept of site-specificity was further reinforced by the recent reexamination of the idea to purchase an autonomous existing work. Artschwager's proposal, on the other hand, was site-specific to a degree beyond that imagined by anyone. However, as the committee examined the model, its strengths became evident, and this unexpected quality ultimately aroused the committee's enthusiasm and wholehearted support.

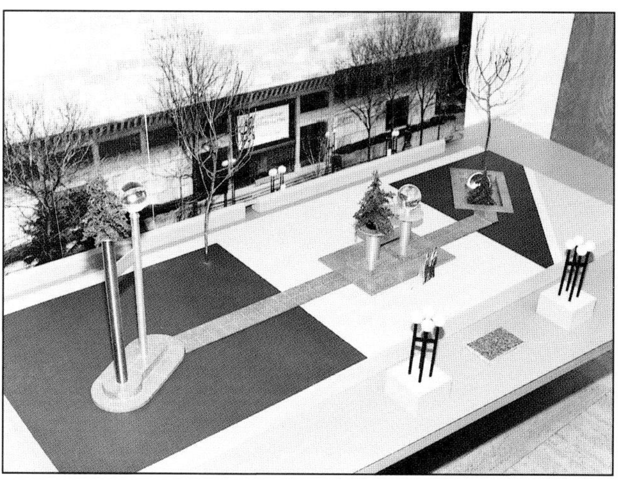

Fig. 1. Model submitted by Richard Artschwager in November 1990

The site for the new sculpture had been loosely identified as the area between permanent concrete planters adjacent to the south facade of the Elvehjem and the existing driveway. The area measures approximately 60×155 square feet (fig. 2). When the building was first constructed, this area was basically a lawn bisected by a 38-foot wide concrete

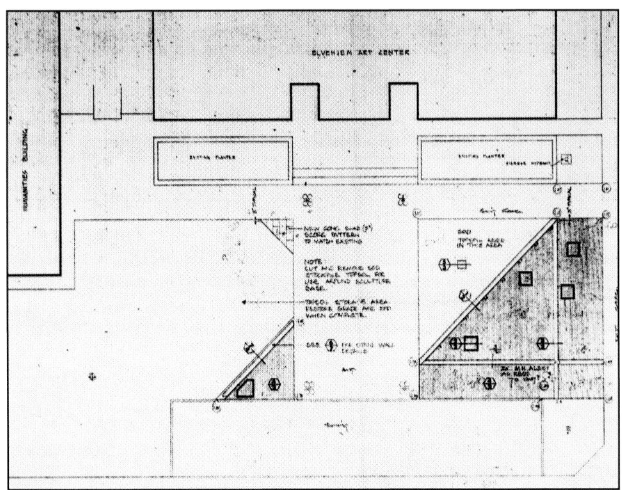

Fig. 2. Site improvement plans, March 14, 1978

walkway leading from the street to the main entrance of the building. In the spring of 1978, a gift from the class of 1928 permitted the planting of trees, and the erection of a large horizontal granite block engraved with the museum's name in the grassy area to the west of the walkway. At the same time, the green tract to the west of the entrance walkway was also embellished; it was subdivided geometrically with paving and the grass was confined to a slightly elevated triangular area contained on the north and west by concrete walkways, while the hypotenuse of the triangle consisted of a retaining wall similar in material and cut to the block engraved with the museum's name. This area was also landscaped with trees, and the recently acquired bronze cast of William Zorach's *Mother and Child,* gift of the Class of 1927, was placed on it highest point. The granite block on the west with the museum's name had been placed diagonally to face motorists traveling east to west on University Avenue. The diagonal wall containing the triangle mound on the east side was aligned parallel to the first granite block and cut from the same color granite in order to unify the site. Following these adjustments, no further changes to the site were made up to the present project.

In its discussions, the Elvehjem sculpture committee had not designated a specific location in the area between the museum's south facade and University Avenue for the placement of the new sculpture. Some consideration had been given to the area closest to the building and immediately to the west of the central walkway, opposite to the Zorach sculpture, an area unused by students or museum visitors. Although it seemed an obvious place for a sculpture, this location was suggested merely as a practical expedient; the committee did not intend to impose a priori limitations on the artist's creativity. Artschwager's model,

however, was a radical departure from expectations since it spread out over the entire area in front of the museum. In conformity with the site, the sculpture was articulated into three distinct sections, one located in the green triangular area to the east, one in the center of the main entrance way itself, and one in the area to the west. Each of the three sections included an evergreen tree and a Plexiglas globe, that, as the artist suggested, would "glow at night like a Japanese lantern." They were to be aligned parallel to the building's facade and, as they progressed from east to west, their components were to increase in height in relation to the flow of one-way vehicular traffic on University Avenue. The lowest section of the sculpture with a half-globe emerging from the ground, would be the first to be perceived by on-coming cars and would not block the view of the succeeding two. The second section occupied the most open space in the area and gently turned away from the street offering a broad face to on-coming traffic, while the third and highest section curved inward toward the street in order to accommodate itself to the alcove created by the conjunction between the Elvehjem and the adjacent Humanities Building. The axis of the eastern and western sections respectively paralleled the low existing granite wall and the granite slab engraved with the museum's name. The tree and globe in the central section were to be raised approximately seven feet above the ground on stainless steel columns; they squarely faced the visitor walking toward the museum's entrance. In the west, the two elements would likewise be raised, except that the columns were to be over twenty feet high. The base of each section was to be red granite.

As attractive and dynamic as these sections and their arrangement were, the Elvehjem sculpture committee was particularly impressed by the strong integration between the sculpture as a whole and the site. The overall design of the sculpture fit so comfortably into its surroundings that the two seemed inseparable. To achieve this effect, Artschwager had incorporated several existing components of the site into his work: the three evergreens duplicated in shape and number those growing in the west section of the area in front of the building; the Plexiglas globes with their metal supporting columns were a somewhat humorous adaptation of the outdoor lights originally designed by the building's architect Harry Weese. A final and unanticipated aspect of the Artschwager proposal, which had great bearing on the committee's positive response, was that it effectively converted the modest area in front of the museum into an attractive public plaza. The Elvehjem, designed in the late 1960s, is an imposing block-like structure whose exterior consists of four unmitigated stone surfaces

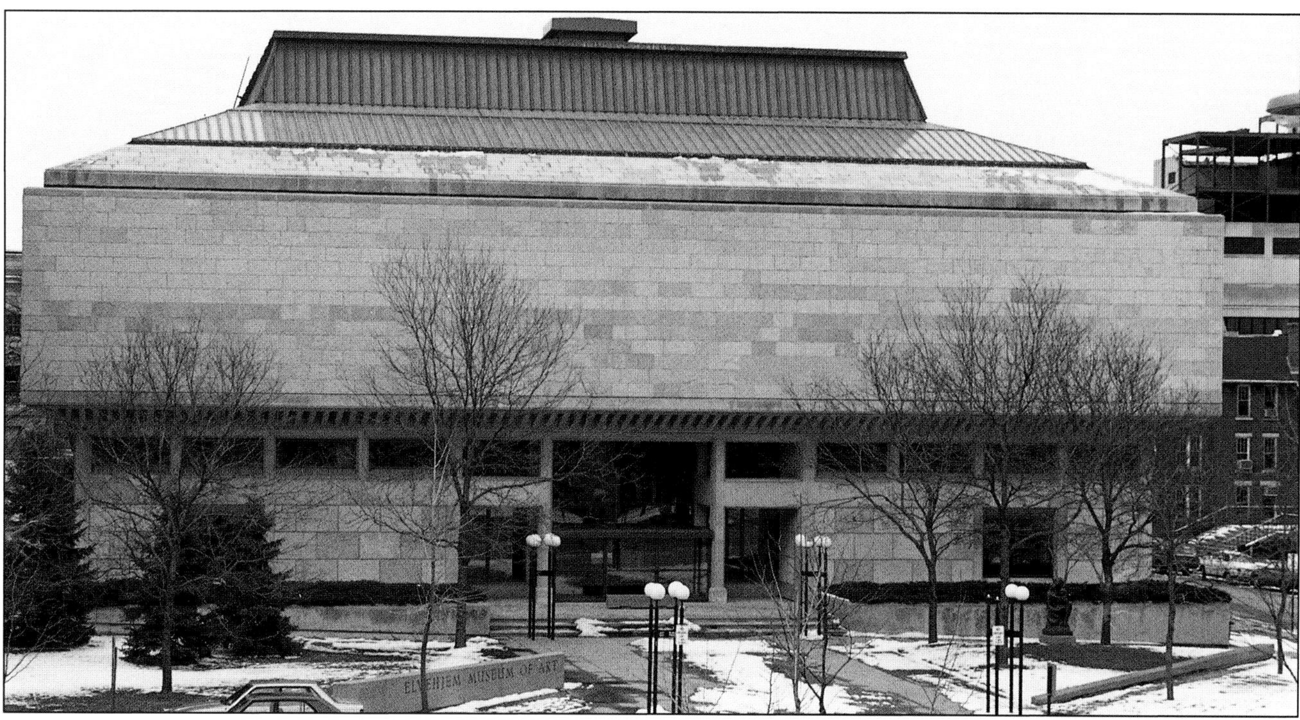

Fig. 3. South facade Elvehjem Museum of Art, 1970

(fig. 3). The immediate impression created by the building is one of reserved dignity, if not actual aloofness. The two granite diagonals created in 1978 by the engraved sign and the retaining wall to embellish the area between the museum and University Avenue, although elegant in intention and material, effectively became additional wall-like barriers between the museum and the community. The Artschwager model not only attracted attention to the museum but by providing elegant seating and a welcoming public space in front of the museum made the building seem less austere and more inviting. This effect promised to be even more convincing at night when the sculpture's lights would illuminate the formerly dark and foreboding area that intervened between the museum and the sidewalk.

The model remained on display in the museum's Paige Court following Artschwager's presentation. Although the museum did not aggressively solicit public response, the committee thought it important to have some sense of how faculty, students, and other visitors to the museum would react. An informal voice poll by the author, other committee members, and the museum's curatorial staff showed an overwhelmingly positive response to the model. Only the survival of the two trees raised on the stainless steel columns, one to a height of more than twenty feet, caused concern; yet everyone recognized the significance of the trees to the overall design of the sculpture. Artschwager's prompt response was to design a system to provide water and nutrients regularly to the raised trees (fig. 4) to allay these fears. Thus, in early August, after only three weeks of "living with the model," as the artist proposed, the Elvehjem sculpture committee enthusiastically endorsed Artschwager's concept and agreed to proceed with the commission pending approval of final drawings.

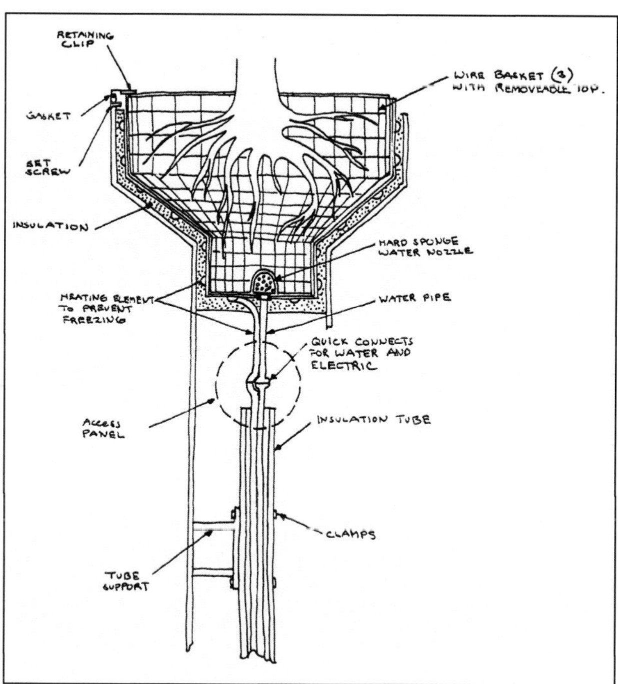

Fig. 4. Proposal for survival of living tree on twenty-two foot column

Artschwager sent the specifications for the sculpture in early November 1990 (figs. 5, 6, 7, and 8). In addition to providing details and dimensions of individual components, the drawings indicated a major change in the design of the eastern section of the sculpture. Originally planned as a granite rectangle enclosing two circles, one containing the tree and one the globe, located within the existing triangle of grass (fig. 9), Artschwager now simplified the geometry of this section, eliminating the rectangle and incorporating the existing triangle directly into the sculpture. The new drawing proposed two enlarged circles contained within a revitalized triangle. The retaining granite wall, marking the hypotenuse of the original triangle erected in 1978, was supplanted with a more accommodating granite seat and was continued around the perimeter of the entire triangle. This modification further enhanced the unity between the site and the sculpture. The question of the trees' survival was also resolved to the committee's satisfaction. The tree situated in the east section of the sculpture would be cared for by the university's grounds department, while the one in the central section, which was accessible from ground level, would be cared for by the nursery under contract to the museum for the maintenance of its indoor plants. The third, and most controversial tree because of its height, would be made of steel and aluminum. In part this was an expedient solution but more important it was in keeping with Artschwager's penchant for comparing the real with the artificial.

The measurements in these drawings afforded some illuminating insights into Artschwager's approach to the design of the Elvehjem sculpture. At first glance, the work seemed abstract and predominantly geometric in conception. However, further examination showed that, in some instances, the measurements, shapes, and alignment of the components of the sculpture were derived directly from elements of the site itself. The triangle which constitutes the base of the eastern section reiterates the triangle that was there before, only now it was energized by a distinctive granite perimeter. The longitudinal axis of the blp-shaped base of the western section parallels the existing granite slab engraved with the name of the museum. Measurements of several components

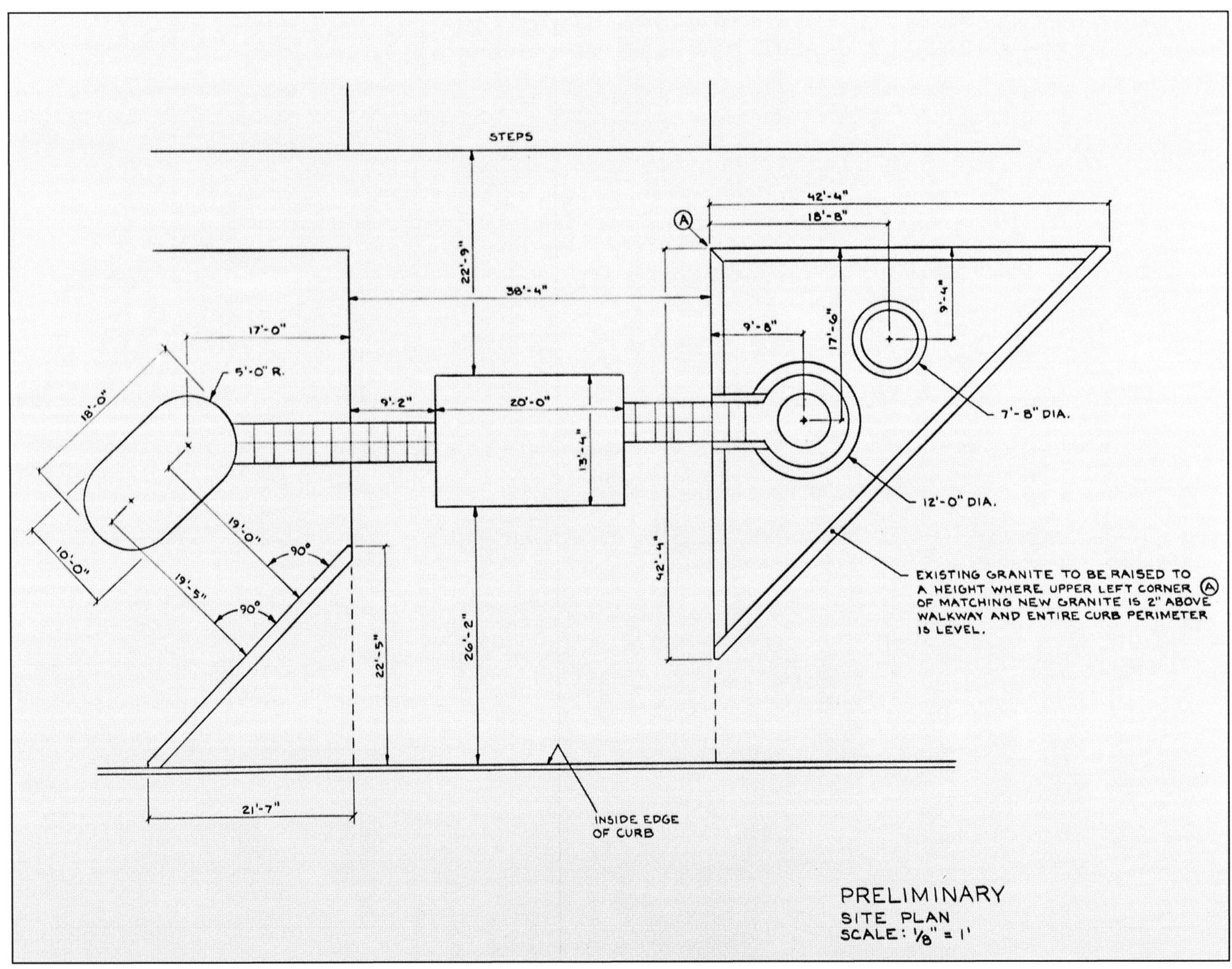

Fig. 5. Preliminary site plan

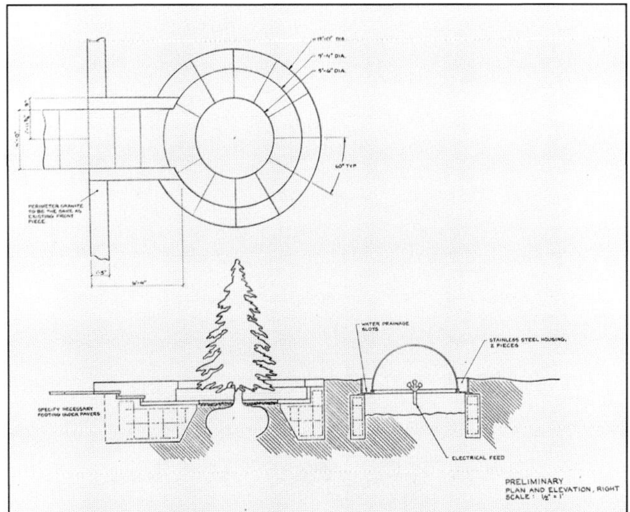

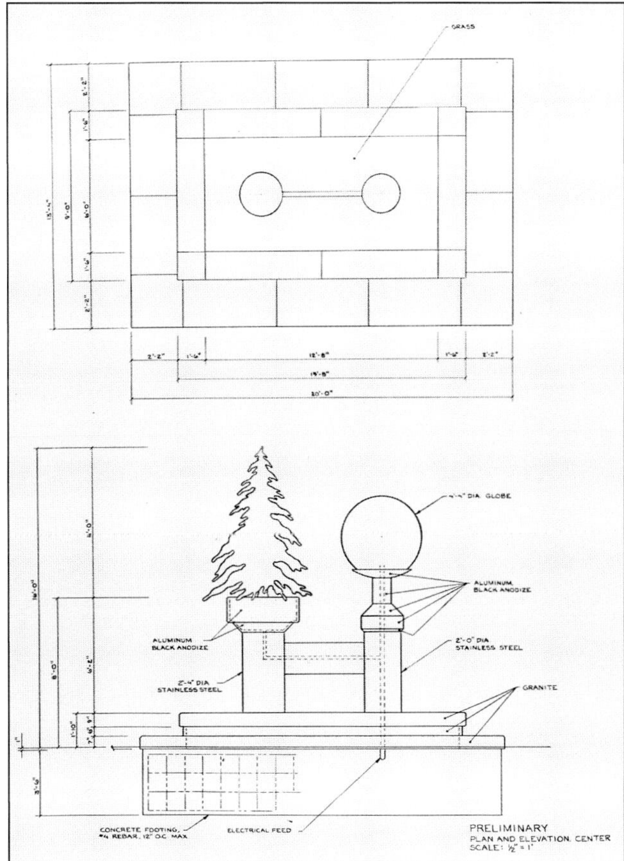

Fig. 6. Preliminary plan and elevation, right

Fig. 7. Preliminary plan and elevation, center

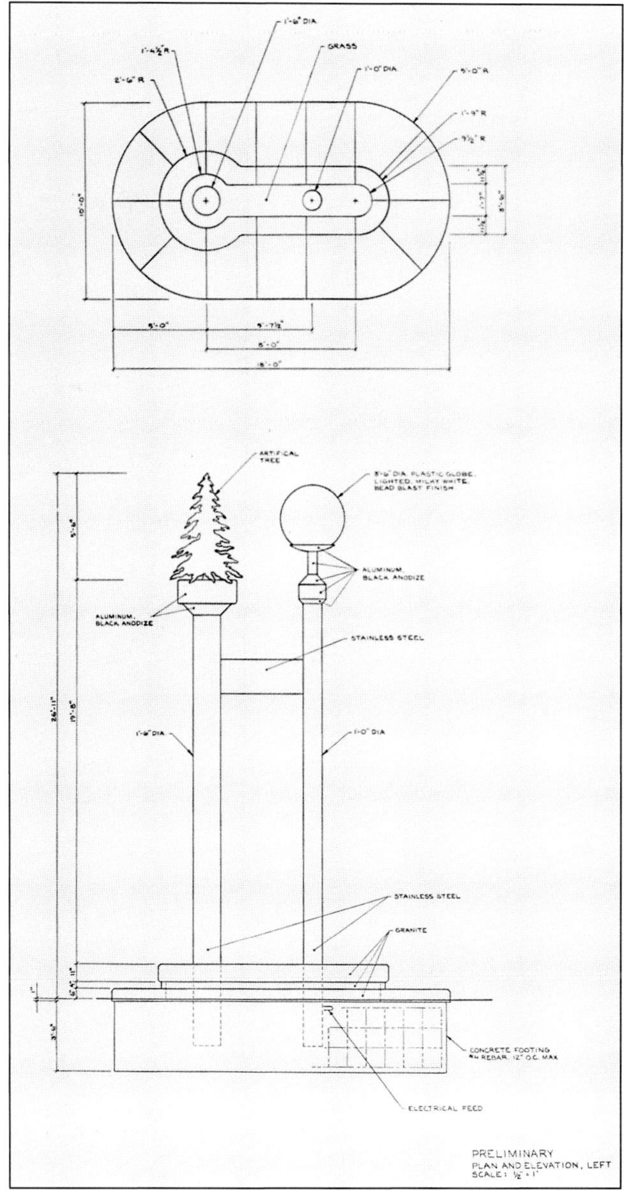

Fig. 8. Preliminary plan and elevation, left

seemed to be based on purely mathematical proportions. The length and width of the granite base in the central section displayed a ratio of 2:3, while the proportion between the height of the tree and its height from the ground in the central section was 1:1. The three Plexiglas globes, from east to west, measure 72 inches, 52 inches and 42 inches, a proportional relationship of 7:5:4, which, to extrapolate further, presents a 2:1 relationship between the first two

globes and the second two globes. However, other measurements proved to be intuitive and based on the artist's imaginative eye and creative experience, or as he put it: "do they seem right." Although the trees and the Plexiglas globes of the sculpture become progressively smaller the more they are elevated above the ground, and the mass of the base for each of the three sections is inversely proportional to its height, there is no discernable mathematical bases for these relationships. In fact, certain key measurements, as for example, the height of the tree in the east section, are not included in the drawings, suggesting that the height was to be determined empirically as the sculpture approached completion.

Shortly after their receipt, the Elvehjem sculpture committee unanimously accepted the drawings Artschwager submitted in November 1990 and

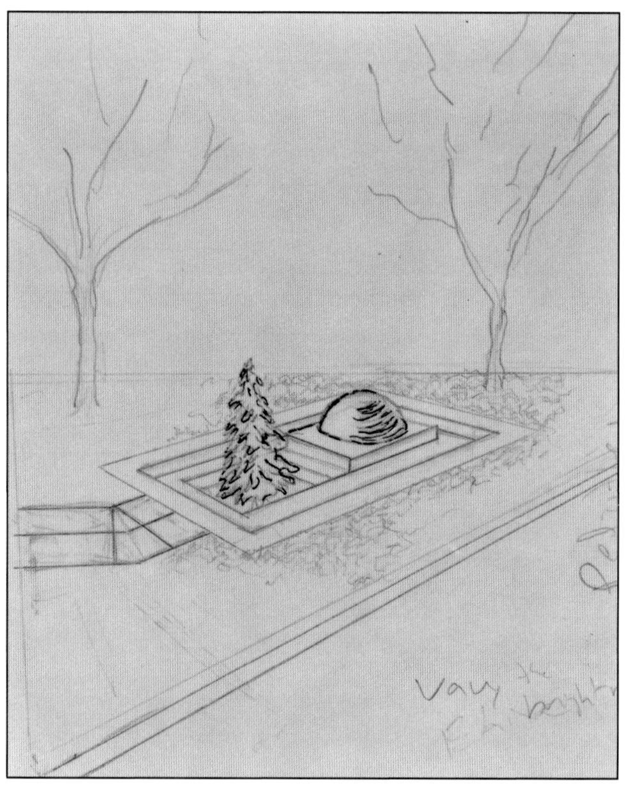

Fig. 9. Preliminary sketch from artist's notebook (1990) showing first concept for east section of sculpture

agreed to proceed with the commission the following spring. It also readily approved the renovation of the central walkway itself, which was unsightly and treacherous after twenty years of wear and weather. Once this was agreed, Artschwager requested that the pattern of interlocking rectangles, each measuring two by four feet, with which the concrete walkway had originally been scored, be replaced with a grid of squares measuring two by two feet. The exact alignment of the square pattern was to be determined by the interstices between the granite tiles of the walkways interconnecting the three sections of the sculpture. For the committee, the appeal of this last suggestion lay in the fact that it too would further enhance the consolidation of the sculpture with the site. Also, it must be confessed that for the art historians on the committee, the new pattern on the concrete walkway and the precise relation of the sculpture to this grid, was tantalizingly reminiscent of Renaissance perspective.

The contract between Richard Artschwager and the Elvehjem Museum of Art was drawn up in the early months of 1991. The committee accepted the ''preliminary'' drawings provided by the artist in November 1990 as final; no significant alterations were to be made without the express approval of the committee. The construction and installation of the sculpture were to be shared: the artist was responsible for the fabrication of the steel, granite, and

Plexiglas elements of the sculpture and for their safe delivery and installation; the Elvehjem would be responsible for all site preparation, which included the necessary concrete footings, and would assist in the installation by providing a crane and two professional riggers at the appointed time. Furthermore, the museum, through the auspices of the university's Department of Planning and Construction, would review all construction plans and advise on structural stability, electrical connections, and overall durability. Site preparation was scheduled to begin in June 1991; the steel and granite were to be delivered and installed in late July 1991.

The Elvehjem sculpture committee recognized the artist's right to make subsequent adjustments in details without full committee review. Artschwager, in fact, continued to test the visual effectiveness of his measurements and surface finishes throughout and after the contract negotiations by building full-scale models of individual components in his studio. As a result of these experiments, Artschwager decided to ''float'' the base of the central section one inch above the concrete walkway rather than setting it directly on it, determined the final relationship between the height and size of the granite perimeter surrounding the eastern triangle and the central walkway, and designed the details for the stairs leading from the central walkway into the circular east well destined to contain the largest tree.

In these last stages of the project, Artschwager also decided on the finishes for the granite components. In July of 1990, together with his model, he had submitted a sample of a Canadian rose colored granite called Lac du Bonnet that was highly polished. As a result of his experiments during the early winter months of 1991, he changed to a muted thermal finish. This decision, by eliminating the strong contrast between the dark glossy color of a polished granite surface and the matt, pebbled surface of the sand-blasted concrete walkway, as well as between the polished granite and the muted thermal finish of the existing carnelian granite block engraved with the museum's name, enhanced the unity between the site and the sculpture. Also, Artschwager replaced the existing red granite wall on the east side of the central walkway, which he had originally planned to extend around the entire perimeter of this triangular area, with Sierra white granite. The use of this second color recognized the preexistence of the triangular area and eliminated the discrepancy between the existing carnelian granite wall installed in 1978 and the Lac du Bonnet granite that Artschwager had selected for his sculpture.

Construction of the Elvehjem sculpture began one month later than originally scheduled. Although the design for the sculpture proper, that is, those parts which would be visible, was basically complete in November 1990, the plans for technical and mechanical aspects of the sculpture which had no aesthetic function, proved more difficult to develop. Climatic conditions and local building codes, rather than the artist, had to dictate the design of the concrete footings. Electrical power, which was to be supplied from the site also proved a complex issue: the artist knew the visual effect that he required from the three Plexiglas globes and could determine the kind of illumination that would produce it; however, he could not determine power requirements or design the necessary conduits. Furthermore, the structural integrity of the six-thousand pound stainless steel columns that would project to a height of over twenty feet and their relative weight-bearing capacities required engineering expertise. Problems that involved technical specialization, which understandably were outside of the artist's normal range of activities, required additional time to solve.

Throughout the negotiations, as well as in the final contract, there was understood a demarcation between the concept of the work of art and its fabrication and installation. Although the contract between Artschwager and the museum stipulated that he would provide complete plans for the sculpture, the artist focused his personal creative energies primarily on the visual aspects of the piece and its aesthetic integration with the site. He delegated the resolution and design of technical and structural details to his business and studio manager Tom MacGregor. MacGregor researched and drew the plans for the concrete footings and elicited designs from various expert sources for the electrical and mechanical connections required for the ultimate assembly of the piece.

Throughout the project MacGregor served as the liaison between the artist and the museum and between the artist and the assorted contractors responsible for fabrication and construction of the various components of the sculpture. MacGregor was in a unique position: after more than five years of collaboration with the artist, he was intimately acquainted with the Artschwager's work; he had the inclination and the technical and communicative skills necessary to coordinate the construction of a work as logistically complex as *Generations*. On the artist's behalf, MacGregor researched and organized the fabrication of the granite sections, the Plexiglas globes, the stainless steel columns, and the artificial tree. He also worked directly with the university's Department of Planning and Construction, Physical Plant, and the contractors engaged by the museum to prepare the site. MacGregor returned to Madison

regularly to review details of construction and to coordinate the actual installation. Although Artschwager made several visits to Madison after the drawings were approved, he did so to satisfy himself on the aesthetic effectiveness of the work in progress.

Work on the site began in early July 1991. The first task was to relocate the bronze *Mother and Child* by William Zorach to the small plaza facing the north facade of the museum which has proved a far superior location for this popular sculpture since it is no longer hidden by the dense foliage. The same day that Zorach's sculpture was removed, the Joe Daniels Construction Company, which was awarded the state contract for concrete work during fiscal 1991, began working on the site. Progress was delayed on two occasions when the artist, who was still conducting studio experiments even at this late date, made several alterations which required the dimensions of the concrete footings to be adjusted. Tom MacGregor, Jim Thomas, general manager of the Joe Daniels Company, and the university's engineers who served as consultants throughout the project, had to redesign and adjust several details. These changes proceeded smoothly since the contributing principals had developed mutual respect and were equally enthusiastic about Artschwager's creation. To accommodate these changes, the prefabricated forms for the footings had to be revised on site, sections of poured and hardened concrete had to be removed, and others added. In spite of these adjustments, site preparation was completed in the allotted six weeks.

A comment about advance scheduling might prove of practical interest. Original forecasts, which were abstractly developed by Tom MacGregor and the author, anticipated that site preparations and installation would require six weeks, beginning in late May and ending in late June of 1991. In order to allow for unforseen circumstances, the unveiling of the new work was delayed to coincide with the opening of *PUBLIC (public)*, an exhibition of Artschwager's work, in mid September. However, the two and a half months, which at first were considered a generous cushion between the work's installation and its inauguration, quickly disappeared. Completion of the technical drawings alone delayed the beginning of the work until early July. The two weeks originally projected for site preparation did not allow for the complexity and massive scale of the footings or the time necessary for curing the concrete. The Joe Daniels Company, once the contract was awarded, immediately adjusted the schedule for site preparation to a more realistic six weeks. Granite installation, originally allotted two to three days, actually required ten. This projection, too, was only read-justed when the contractor arrived on site. Only the installation of the stainless steel columns was finished in the one day originally allotted. The work could not be scheduled more exactly because both the museum and the artist lacked prior experience with a project that required such extensive site preparation. The contractors, who ultimately were the best source of information, could not develop a realistic work schedule until they actually were awarded the con-tract. Thus the two-and-a-half month contingency period allowed by the museum between the expected completion of the sculpture and the unveil-ing, which originally seemed embarrassingly long, turned out to be essential.

The Cold Spring Granite Company of Minne-sota delivered the granite and began its installation on August 5, two days after the completion of the concrete footings and pavement. Artschwager had selected this particular vendor because of its prior experience with sculpture; Cold Spring Granite had provided the stone for several of the works in the Walker Art Center's recently created sculpture gar-den in Minneapolis, and they had cut and installed the granite for *Oasis,* a commission Artschwager had just completed for the General Mills Corporation, also in Minneapolis. In addition, their proximity to Madison promised lower transportation costs. The installation of the granite, as complex as it was because of the circular shapes involved, proceeded smoothly with only two brief delays. In the first instance, when the center of the concrete footing for the circle that was to contain the tree in the east sec-tion of the piece was found to be displaced by one inch, the position of the individual granite blocks in this area had to be recalculated so the interstices would line up in the manner designed by the artist. The second problem was similar: the central concrete walkway, with its square grid pattern had, for the sake of expediency, been poured at the same time as the footings. The interstices between the granite blocks did not line up with the grid lines which had been scored on the concrete. To solve this problem, the contractor removed the concrete squares directly adjacent to the granite and repoured and rescored them after the granite blocks were assembled.

Mison, Inc. of Rochester, New York, manufac-tured and installed the stainless steel components and the Plexiglas globes. These were delivered preassem-bled on Tuesday, August 20, and installed in a single day. This part of the project, too, was not without complications. The day before delivery, it was dis-covered that the diameter of the rim at the base of the twenty-two foot columns was two inches too large to fit between the granite blocks constituting its base. Although the concrete footings beneath the granite had been notched to accommodate the sup-porting rim, the granite blocks once installed, restricted access to this opening. For installation of the sculpture to proceed, the one-inch thick stainless steel rim either had to be cut down to fit into the existing opening—no easy task—or the granite blocks had to be removed. Again, the university's Physical Plant came valiantly to the rescue. Although it had never been tested, the department owned a plasma-cutter which, according to the manufacturer's specifica-tions, could cut through one-inch thick stainless steel. Immediately upon arrival, the truck from Rochester was redirected to the mechanical shop where the plasma-cutter lived up to its reputation. The steel components were returned to the installation site; the university's electricians completed the wiring in the columns. For the installation itself, the museum hired a crane and two professional riggers from the locally based Reynolds Company and, under the supervision of Tom MacGregor, the sculpture was assembled with no further mishaps.

In the last phase of the installation, the Bruce Company of Middleton, Wisconsin, planted the two blue Colorado spruce trees which were part of the sculpture and landscaped the site. The two living trees, which Artschwager had selected during an earlier visit, measured twelve feet and eight feet in height. The larger of the two was easily planted in the granite circle located in the triangular east section of the sculpture, the smaller was laboriously hoisted into the stainless steel container atop its eight-foot column which had been completely filled with earth to give the roots the opportunity to expand down-wards. The container was lined with electrical heat tape which would be activated during the winter months to keep the root ball from freezing. According to Artschwager's design, the twelve-foot tree would eventually to grow to an ideal height of between fif-teen and eighteen feet; the tree planted atop the col-umn would remain relatively constant in size due to the constraints imposed on its root expansion by the container. In any event, should either tree become too large, it could be replaced. Artschwager's design also called for placing a hedge of yews just behind and along the whole length of the granite block engraved with the museum's name, so that people sitting on the blp-shaped western section of the sculp-ture would be pleasantly enclosed within a green area. The Bruce Company also provided the soil and sodding for the three grassy areas, one in each sec-tion of the sculpture. The two small areas immediately around the columns in both the blp-shaped base to the east and the rectangular base in the center were to be flat; the large green area contained within the granite triangle to the east, was given an irregular undulating surface. The color of these three areas served as a unifying factor for the various sections of the sculpture and replaced, during the hours of bright sunlight, the contrasting color that the sculpture lost when the polished granite surface was abandoned in favor of a matt finish.

The third tree, Artschwager had decided earlier on in the project, would be artificial. He shared the responsibility for its creation with his colleague Tom MacGregor and, together, they studied how to make a realistic-looking tree which would be able to survive the harsh climate. While an artificial tree would not require nutrients or water, it faced the hazards of strong winds, ice and snow, and blistering summer heat. After studying alternatives and consulting with technicians, they fabricated the tree from stainless steel and aluminum. It consisted of an irregular hollow stainless steel tube on which marine epoxy was built up, stippled, and later ground out with a Dremel tool to simulate tree bark. Branches extended from this vertical core; each one was a series of telescoping aluminum tubes, pierced with thousands of aluminum pins bent to resemble pine needles. Although the materials used as well as the sectional construction of the branches would give the tree a certain amount of flexibility to resist a strong wind and to give way under the weight of snow, the artist also placed a warm air blower in the supporting stainless column where it joined with the base of the tree. During the winter it would supplement the heat tapes by blowing warm air at regular intervals up through the trunk of the tree and out through the hollow branches. The tree's colors, which completed the illusion of reality,

were provided by several coats of DuPont Imron, a highly durable paint used by the trucking and aircraft industries.

As the sculpture approached completion, Artschwager named it *Generations.* Earlier on, he had experimented with other titles: first *Two Times Three,* responding to the compositional rhythm of two paired elements, a tree and a globe, multiplied three times, but later discarded it as obvious and bland. For a time he favored *PUBLIC (public),* the title of the exhibition which was organized to introduce his latest work to the Madison community. Artschwager found the relationship between his earlier outdoor works, brought together for the first time in the Elvehjem exhibition, and the new sculpture intriguing and for both to have the same title seemed somehow appropriate. However, ultimately he decided that the relationship between his new and earlier work was better expressed by *Generations,* in the sense of artistic evolution: the new sculpture had been generated by those that preceded it. Furthermore, this word was laden with connotations directly related to the sculpture itself. *Generations* could suggest things brought into being by generation, a process of growth and development, reflected in the emergence from the earth and the gradual reaching upward of the three individual sections of the new sculpture. The three sections could also be seen as three different generations of the same thing, each one reflecting a particular evolutionary stage. Or the three sections, if the paired tree and globe were metaphorically correlated to a human couple, could represent three different generations of a cycle, i.e., three different generations of a family.

In a very real sense, *Generations* evolved from Artschwager's earlier outdoor commissions. These eleven works remain relatively unknown, since they

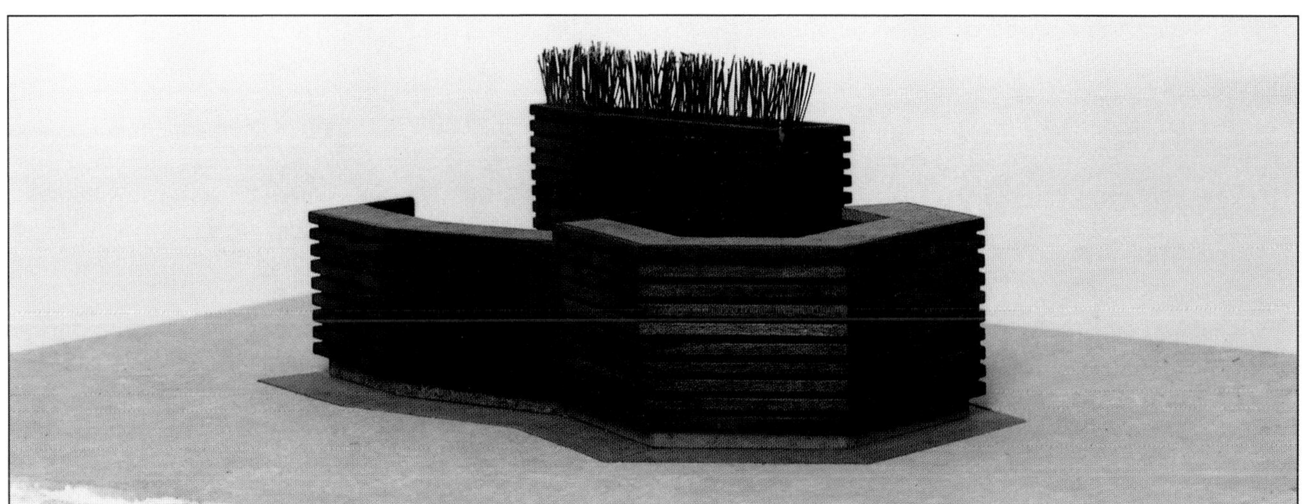

Fig. 10. *Safe Harbor,* 1990, Granite, bronze, ash, maple and grass, 18 × 6 × 12 ft., reception desk and tables for Pacific Enterprises Project, Los Angeles, 1990

were not completed until after his retrospective exhibition at the Whitney Museum of American Art in 1987. Although his first outdoor commission, the concrete tree/ bicycle rack (illus. 3, p. 69) (in Münster, Germany) was conceived and completed the same year of his retrospective, the Seattle County Jail had already approached Artschwager with a request for an outdoor site-specific work in 1982. *Transactions* (illus. 1c, p. 63) today only exists in model form because of a vague resemblance, unintended by the artist, between the installation's central element and a guillotine. Both *Transactions* and the Münster sculpture already prefigured elements and formal qualities of the Elvehjem installation. Like *Generations,* the Seattle County Jail model is articulated into three distinct sections, each of which invites casual audience interaction, while the Münster piece incorporates two living trees raised above ground level. Unlike *Generations,* however, *Transactions* can exist independently from the originally intended site, and may someday be constructed. Each of its components is autonomous in a way that the components of the Elvehjem

sculpture are not. In fact, its central element, with the new title *Counter III* was installed at the foot of Central Park during the winter months of 1988–89 (illus. 1b, p. 64). Also, the Egyptian thrones, originally intended for society's judges in *Transactions,* reappear in an installation entitled *Sitting/Stance,* which Artschwager completed for the West Thames Park in Battery Park City in 1988 (illus. 2d, p. 67). *Sitting/ Stance* also includes a working lamp, whose design is based on the existing street lamps and which can be considered a conceptual forerunner of the illuminated globes in *Generations* (illus. 2e, p. 67), as well as tree in the center of a table (illus. 2f, p. 68). Living trees and grasses also appear incorporated in two very recent works, the already mentioned *Oasis* commissioned by the General Mills Corporation in Minneapolis (illus. 6, p. 70) and an indoor piece, *Safe Harbor,* designed for the Pacific Enterprises Project in Los Angeles, California (fig. 10). Both were completed in 1990.

Drawings in Artschwager's working notebooks shed some additional light on the relation of *Generations* to his earlier outdoor commissions. In one undated but obviously preliminary study in which

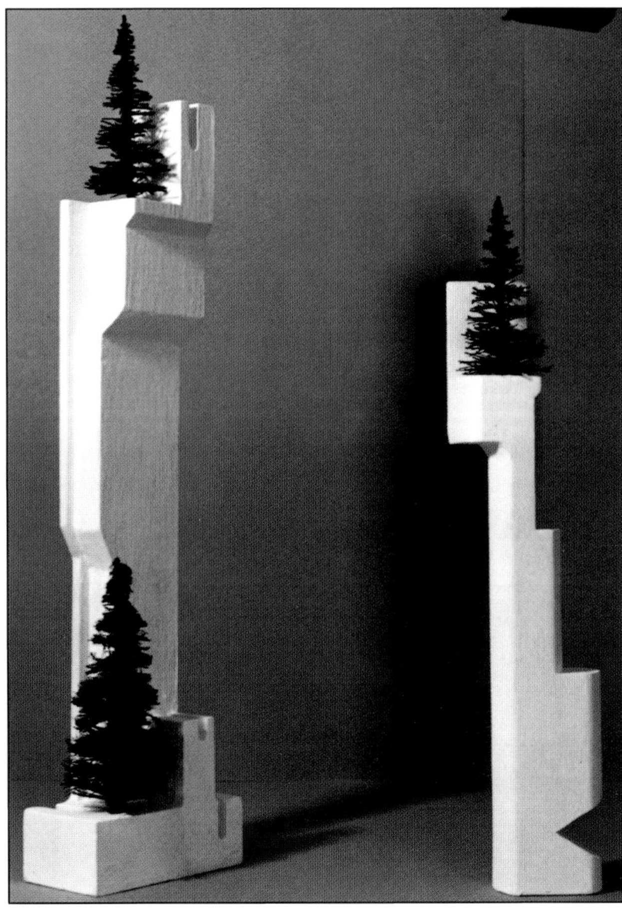

Fig. 12. Model for outdoor sculpture commission for *Skulptur Projekte in Münster,* 1987. Commissioned by Westfalisches Landesmuseum, Münster, Germany

Fig. 11. Preliminary sketch from artist's notebook (1990)

Artschwager already sees the Elvehjem sculpture embracing the central walkway (fig. 11), the vertical element to the left of the walkway bears a strong resemblance to the bicycle rack (fig. 12). Like the 1987 untitled work designed for the city of Münster in Germany, the element in the drawing is tall, solid, and progresses upward in a series of block-like steps. Also like the Münster piece, it supports a tree on top, and a globe, which has replaced the tree in the earlier piece, on a lower projecting ledge. Another drawing (fig. 13) shows the single element with two levels, one for the tree and one for the globe, separated into two distinct vertical elements. However, the one carrying the globe is still vaguely reminiscent of bicycle rack. In a drawing, dated May 29, 1990 (fig. 14), the columns supporting tree and globe already appear in their final form; however, a small sketch to the right still shows a multileveled geometric structure that is somewhat of a cross between bicycle rack and the more recent *Oasis*.

Although Artschwager carries forward several of the ideas he developed in the earlier commissions, in *Generations* he sets out in a bold new direction. The work and the site are inseparable both visually and conceptually; in fact, the concept of site predominates over what is usually understood by the term ''work of art.'' Visitors who have seen the drawings or the conceptual model are able to distinguish the piece from the site but comment that ''it looks like it has always been there.'' On the other hand, visitors, who have no prior knowledge of the piece and have never before seen the site but are brought out to see the museum's new work by Richard Artschwager, are unable to distinguish immediately what the work actually is. This lack of individualistic assertiveness, lack of clearly separating one's own work from that which was there before and which still remains, makes the work a truly public place, one that participates and becomes part of the on-going history of the community; in the final analysis, the sculpture belongs more to the public than it does to the artist.

The incorporation of illuminated globes into the piece enhances the work's integration not only with the site but also with the entire community. White globes were not only used to illuminate the area in front of the Elvehjem when it was first designed but they also appear in front of and attached to the facade of Vilas Hall across the street, in the plaza to the north of the Elvehjem, through the public areas in the adjacent Humanities Building, and all along State Street, the main thoroughfare leading from Bascom

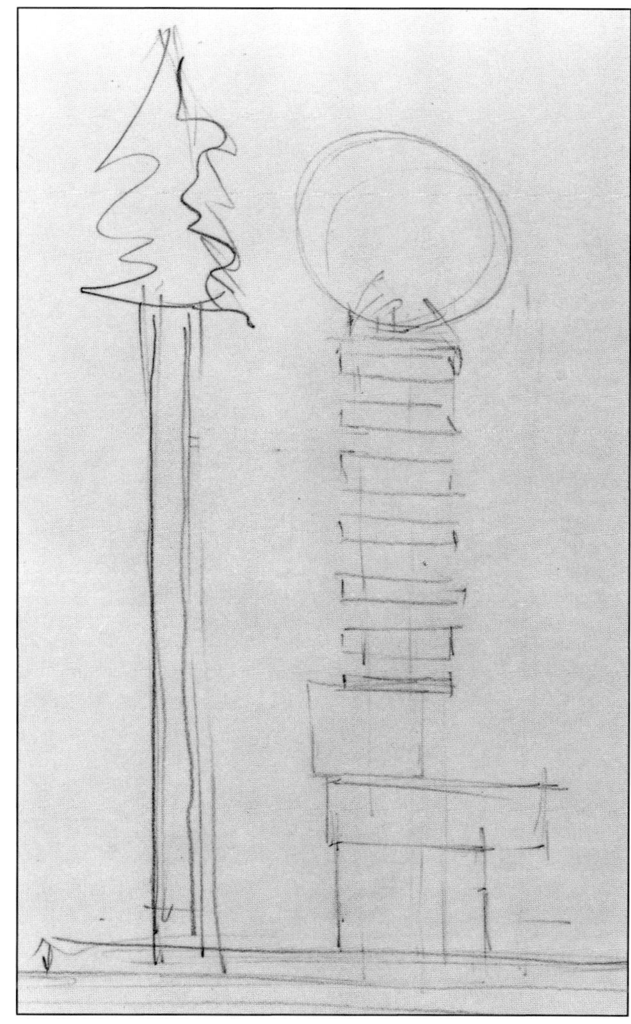

Fig. 13. Preliminary sketch from artist's notebook (1990)

Hall to the State Capital, as well as in many other areas throughout the city. Their presence in such exaggerated size in Artschwager's piece, in a sense, makes the Elvehjem plaza and the main entrance to the museum a focal point for the community.

The Elvehjem inaugurated *Generations* on September 13, 1991. A topping-off ceremony seemed more appropriate than an unveiling given the almost architectural nature of Artschwager's latest creation. Presiding was university Chancellor Donna Shalala who, at the controls of a crane, hoisted the artificial tree to its final seat aloft the twenty-two foot stainless steel column. With this final piece in place, the sculpture was complete.

Russell Panczenko
Director of the Elvehjem Museum of Art
University of Wisconsin–Madison

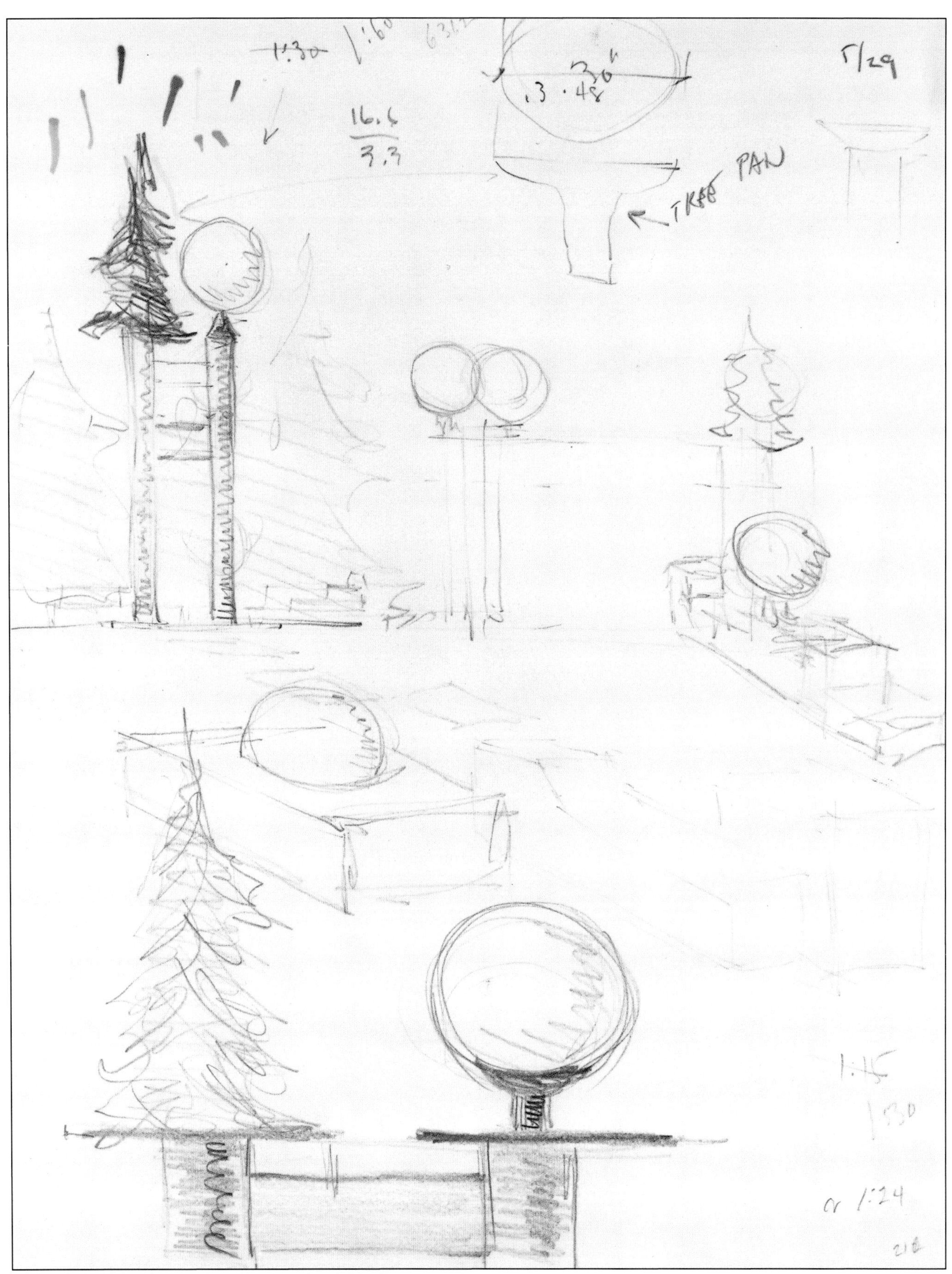

Fig. 14. Preliminary sketch from artist's notebook (29 May 1990)

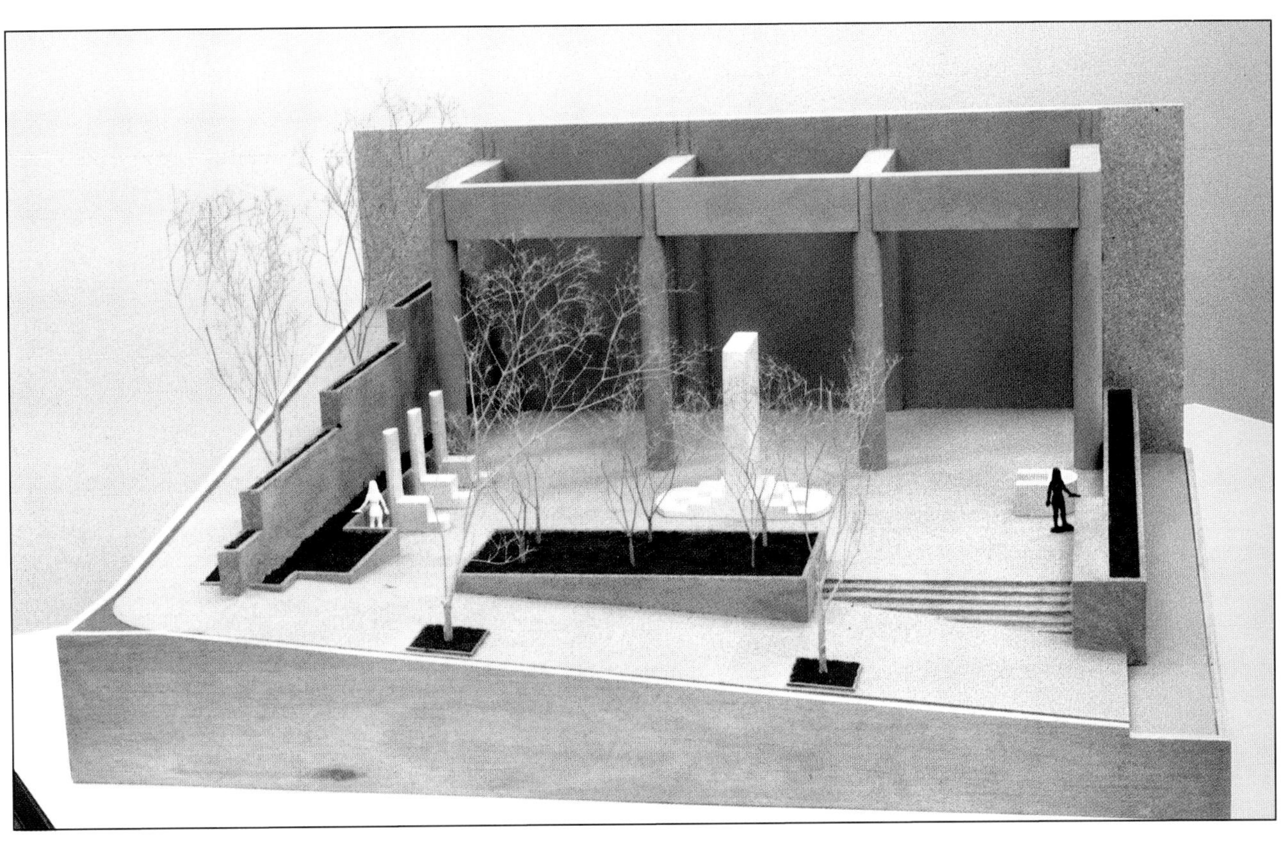

1. *The Transaction*, 1982–89
1a. *The Transaction* (model), 1982, model for unrealized plaza proposal, King County Jail, Seattle, Washington, model destroyed

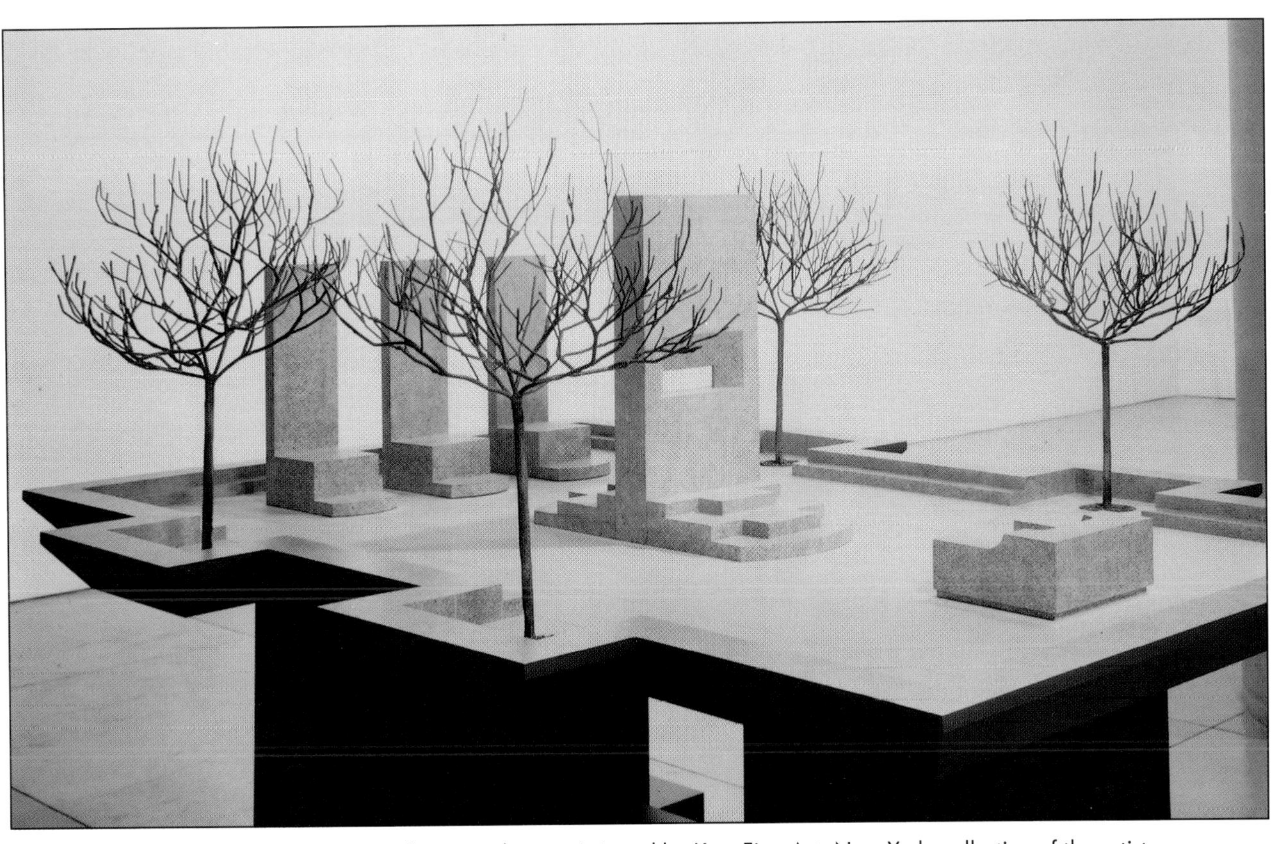

1c. *The Transaction* (model), 1989, revised proposal, commissioned by Kent Fine Art, New York, collection of the artist

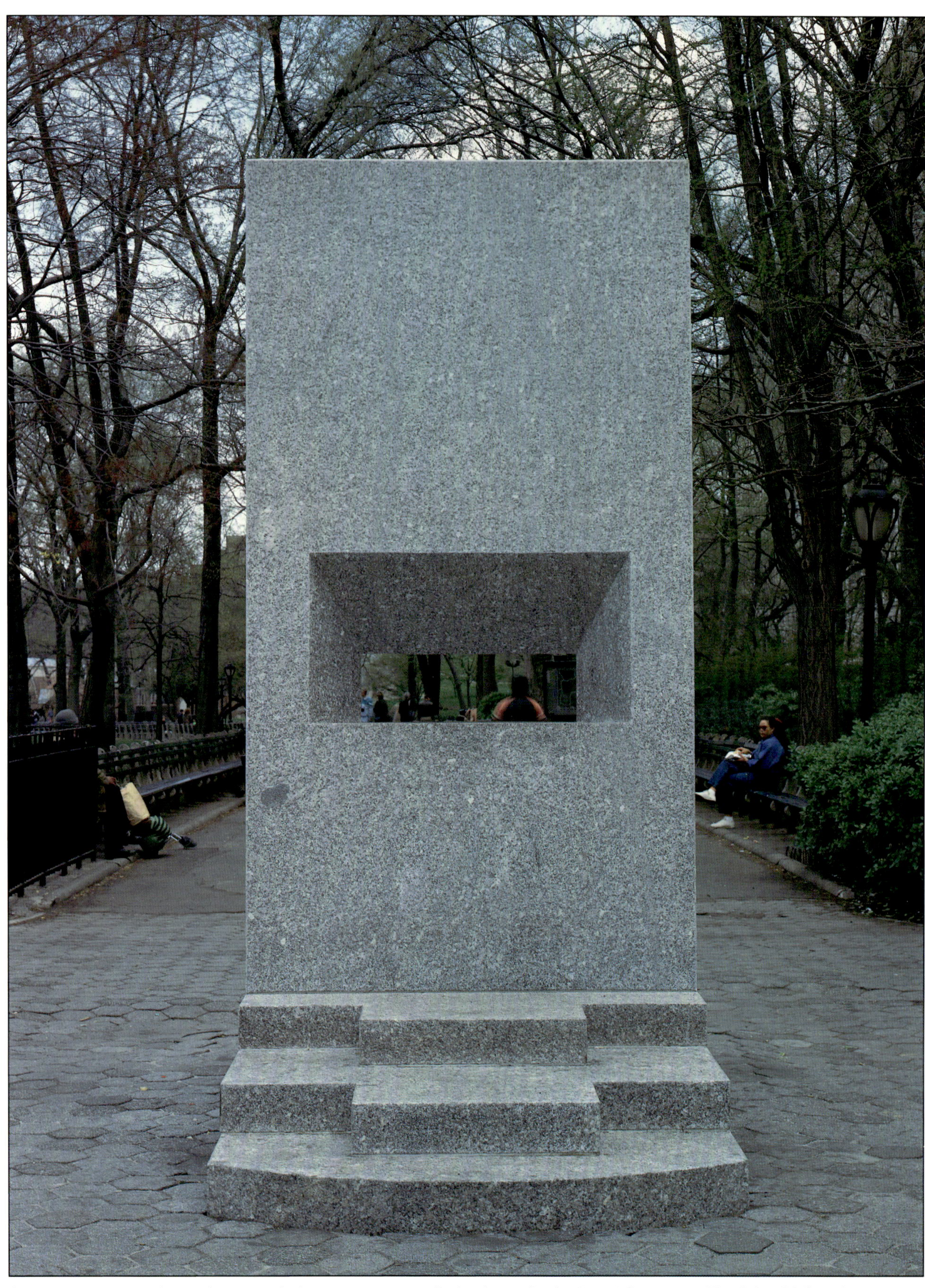

1b. *Counter III,* 1987 (central section of *The Transaction* installed independently, Deer Isle granite, 12 × 5³/₄ × 20 feet, base
13¹/₆ × 5³/₄ feet, on site, December 22–May 23, 1988 (The Public Art Fund), The Doris C. Freedman Plaza, New York, collection
Kent Fine Art, New York

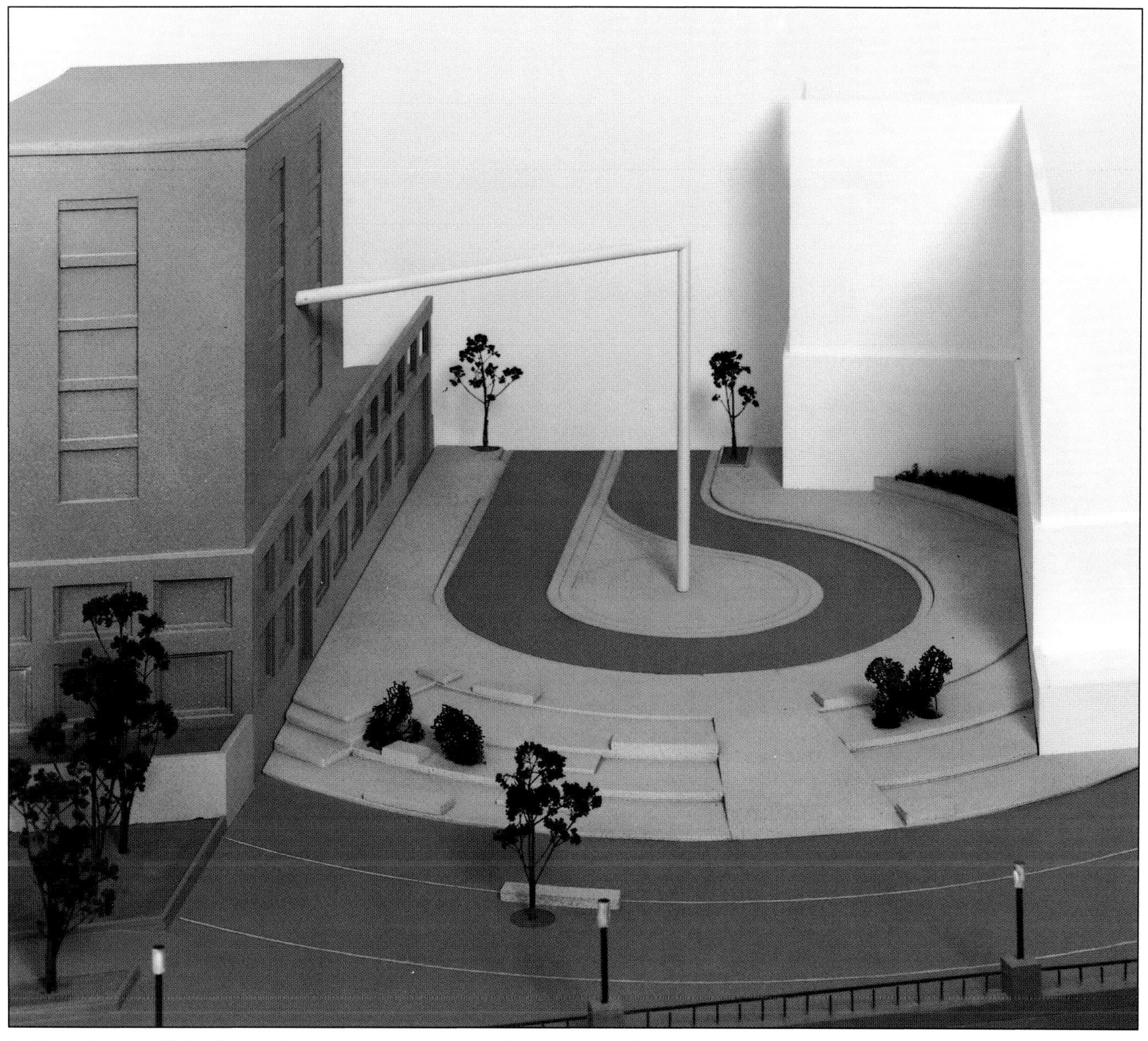

2. *Sitting/Stance,* 1983–88, outdoor sculpture commission for Battery Park City, West Thames Street Park, New York
2a. Preliminary model for proposed sculpture for West Thames Park, December 1983, Battery Park City, New York, collection of
the artist

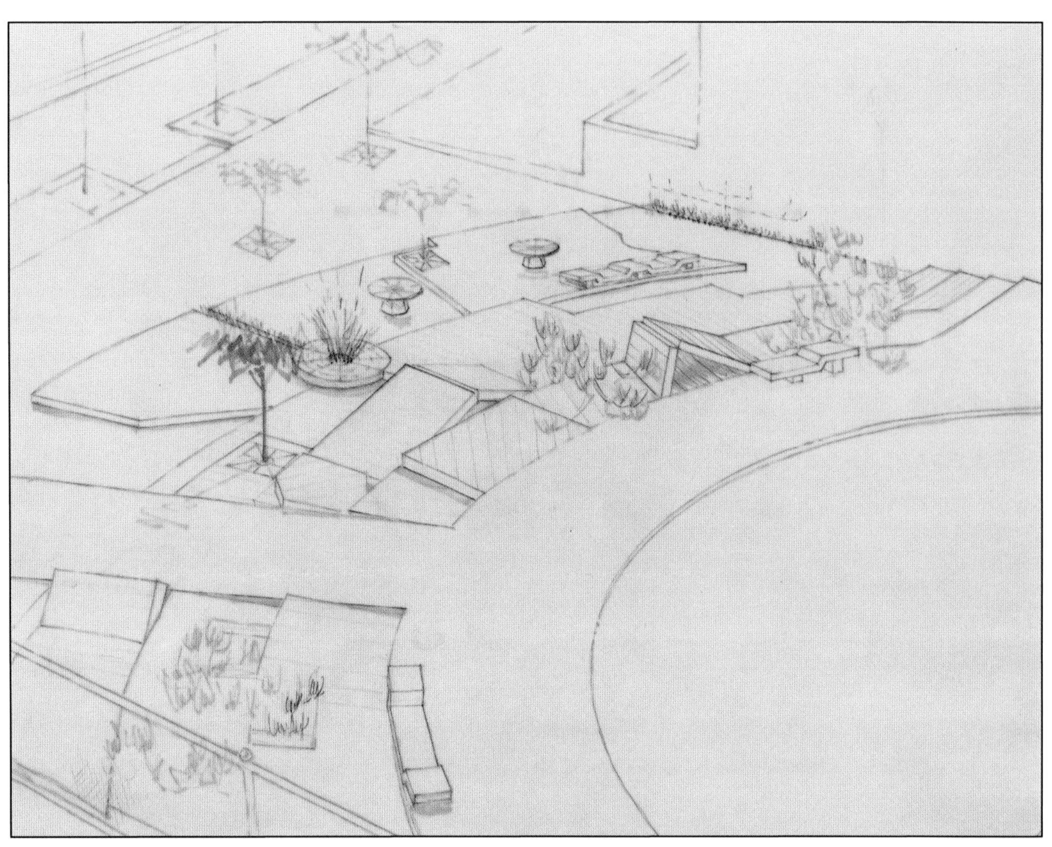

2b. Developmental drawing for proposed sculpture for West Thames Street Park, 1983, Battery Park City, New York, collection of the artist

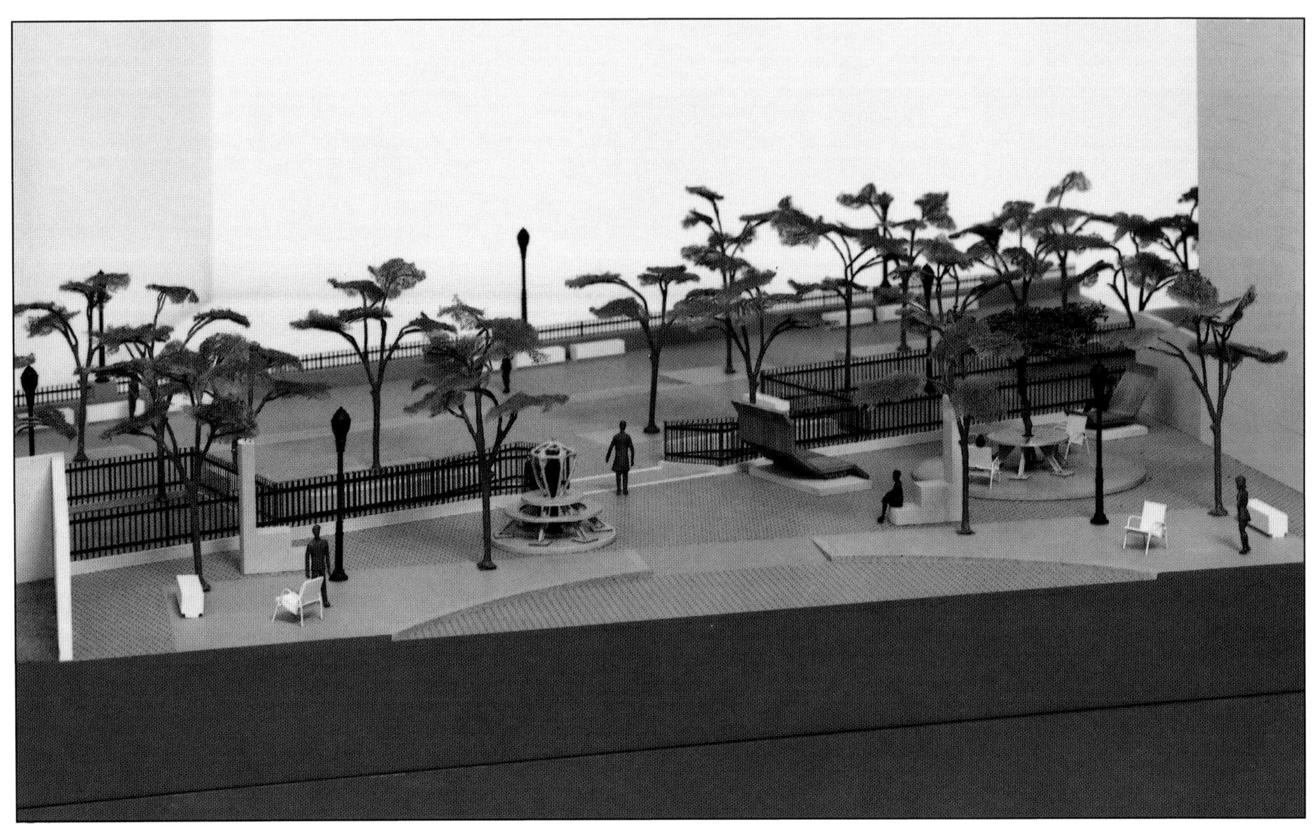

2c. Realized model for sculpture for West Thames Street Park, 1987, Battery Park City, New York, collection of the artist

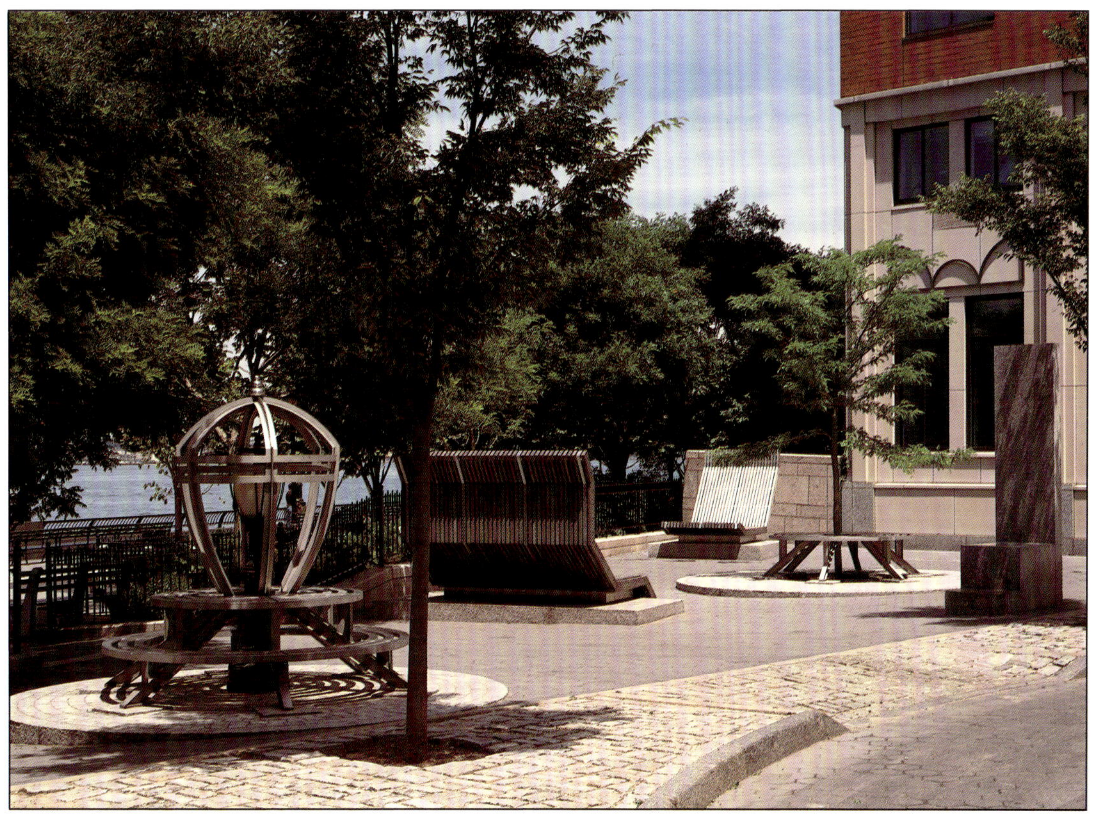

2d. *Sitting/Stance,* outdoor sculpture for West Thames Street Park, completed June 1988, Battery Park City, New York

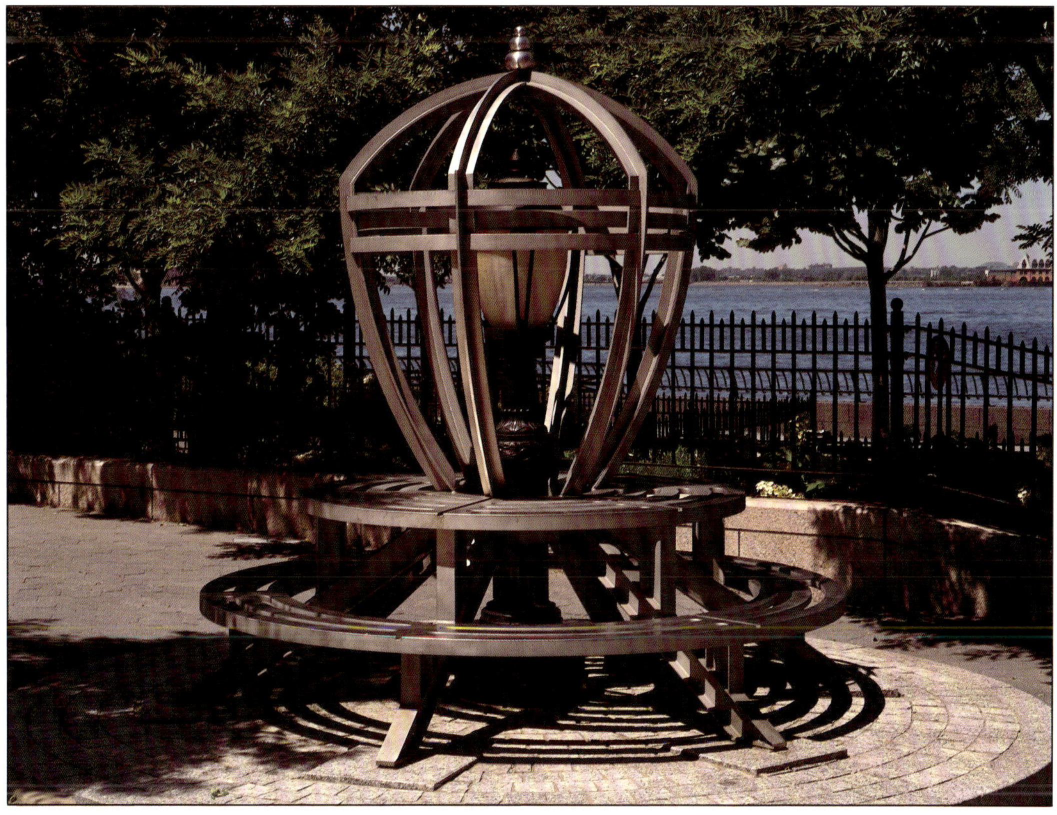

2e. *Sitting/Stance* (detail), stainless steel table, cast iron lamp post and light, 11 feet high × 11 feet diameter, Battery Park City, New York

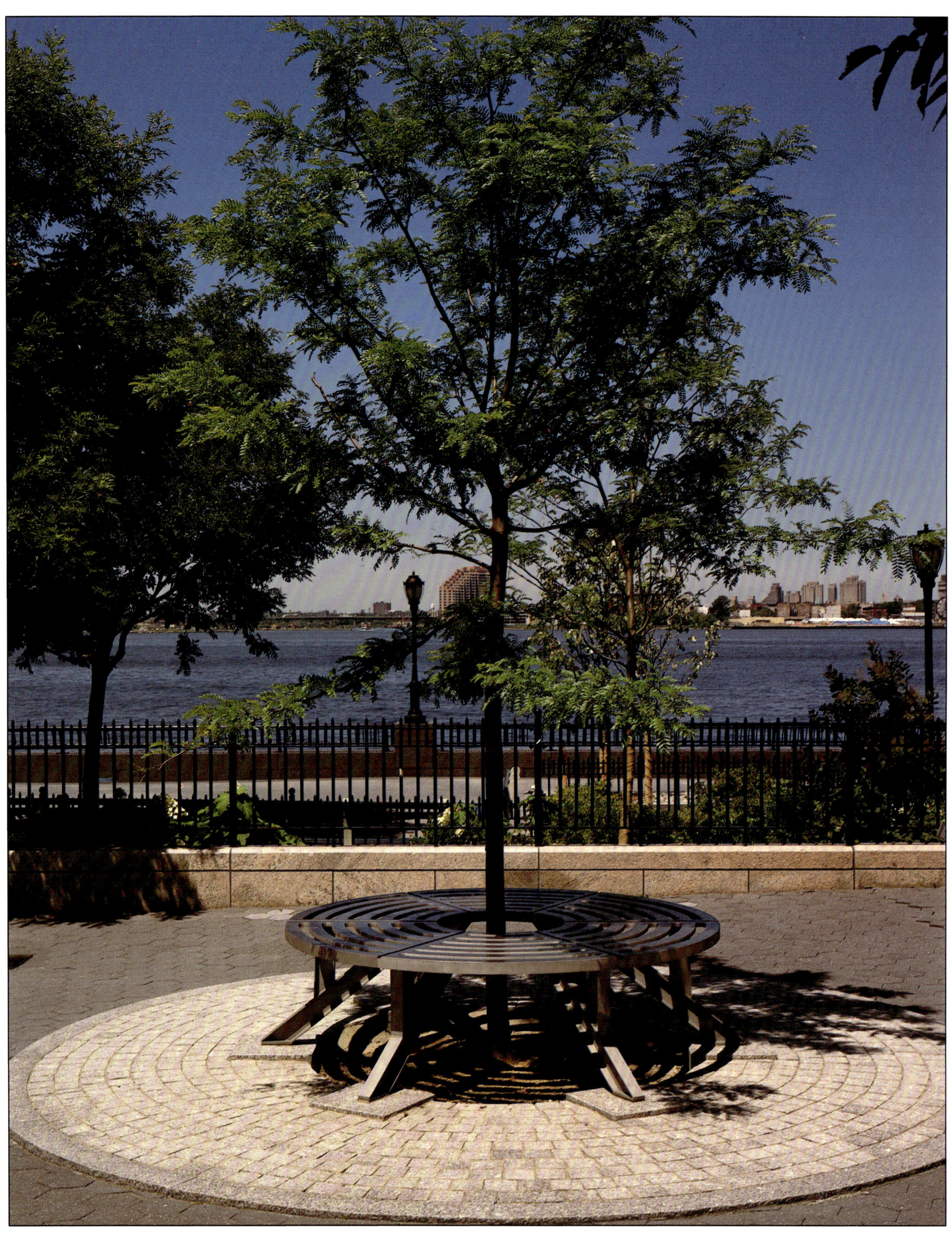

2f. *Sitting/Stance* (detail), stainless steel table and tree, table, $8^{7}/_{12} \times 1^{5}/_{6}$ feet, Battery Park City, New York

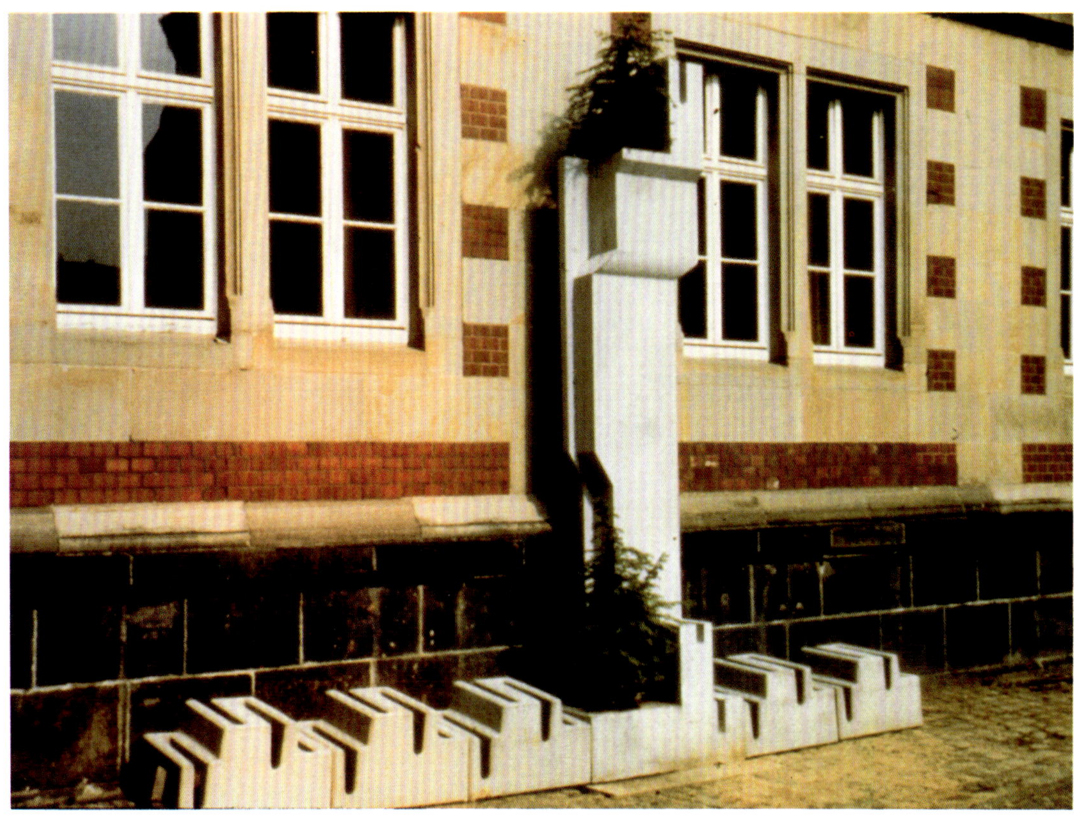

3. Untitled, 1987, concrete and two trees, 11×14×5 feet, outdoor sculpture commission for *Skulptur Projekte in 1987, Münster*, Westfalisches Landesmuseum, Münster, Germany

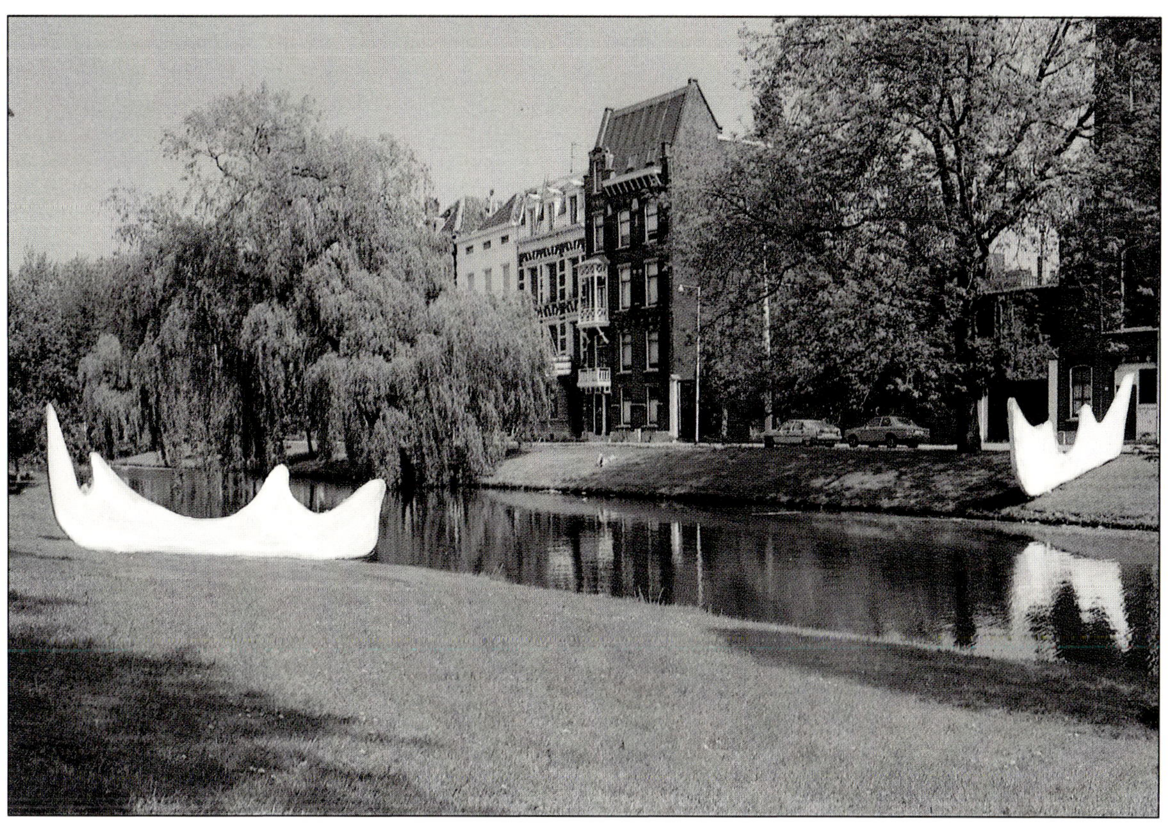

4. Untitled, 1988, concrete, two parts: 7×18½ feet and 7×11½ feet, temporary sculpture commission for *Beelden in de Stad* (Sculpture in the City), by the Museum Buymans–van Beuningen, Rotterdam, Holland

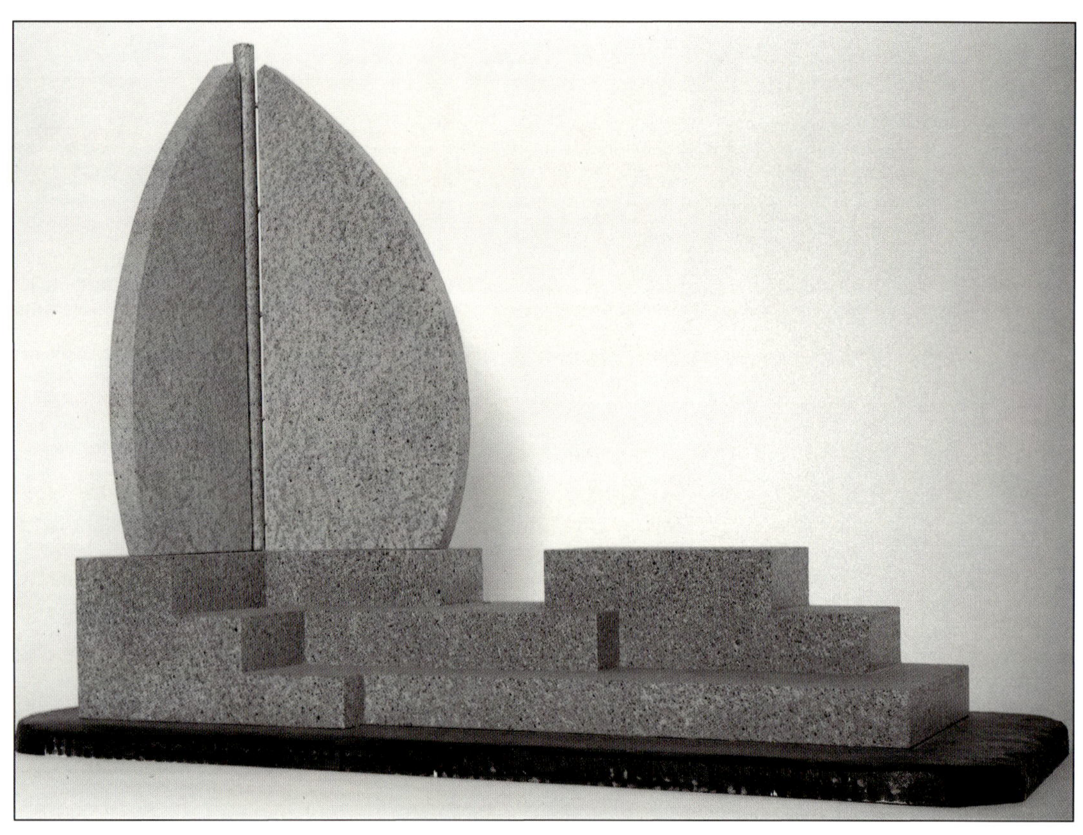

5. *Sails* (model), 1988, granite, 9 1/2 × 10 1/2 × 4 1/2 feet, unrealized proposal, collection of the artist

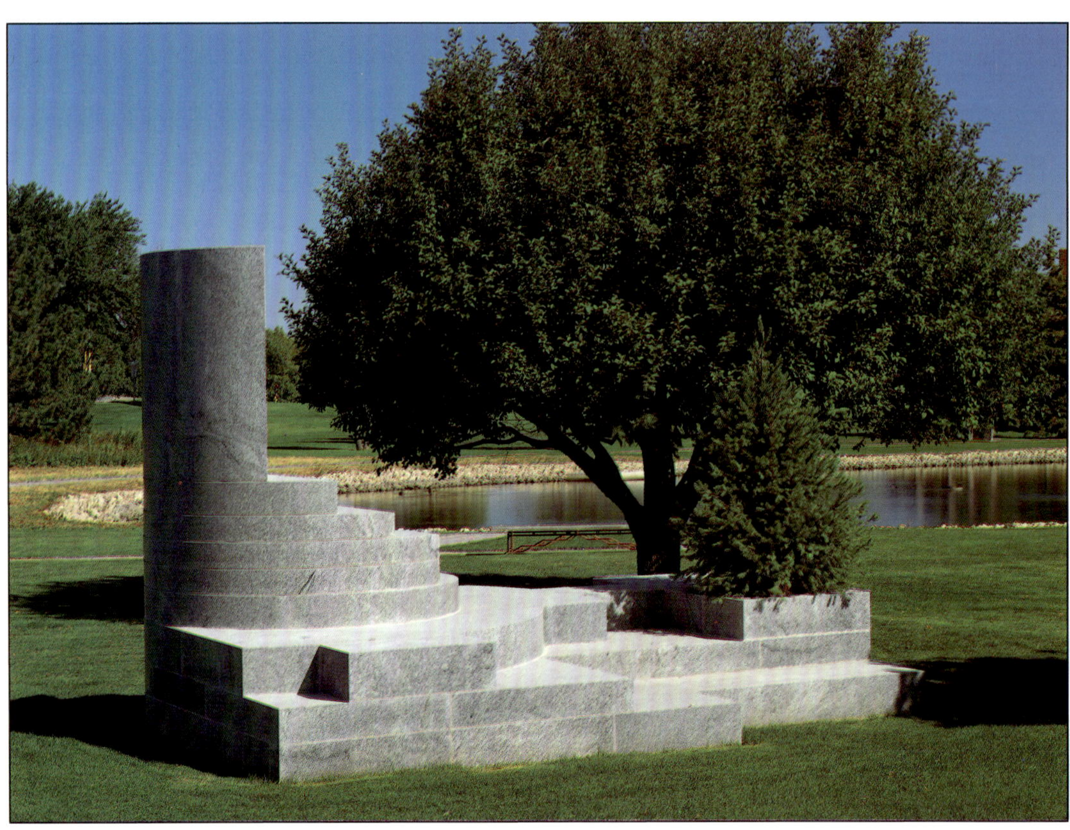

6. *Oasis* , 1988–90, granite and tree, 12 × 18 × 11 feet, General Mills Corporation, Minneapolis, Minnesota

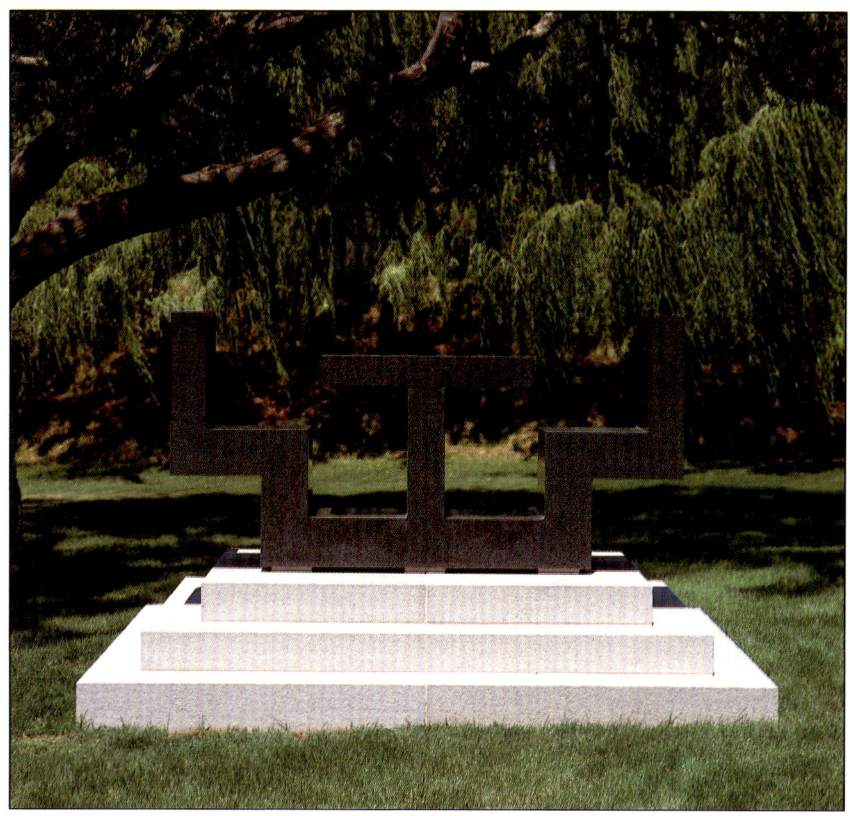

7. *One on One* , 1989, granite, 6 × 10 1/2 × 9 feet, Douglas Cramer
Foundation, Santa Barbara, California

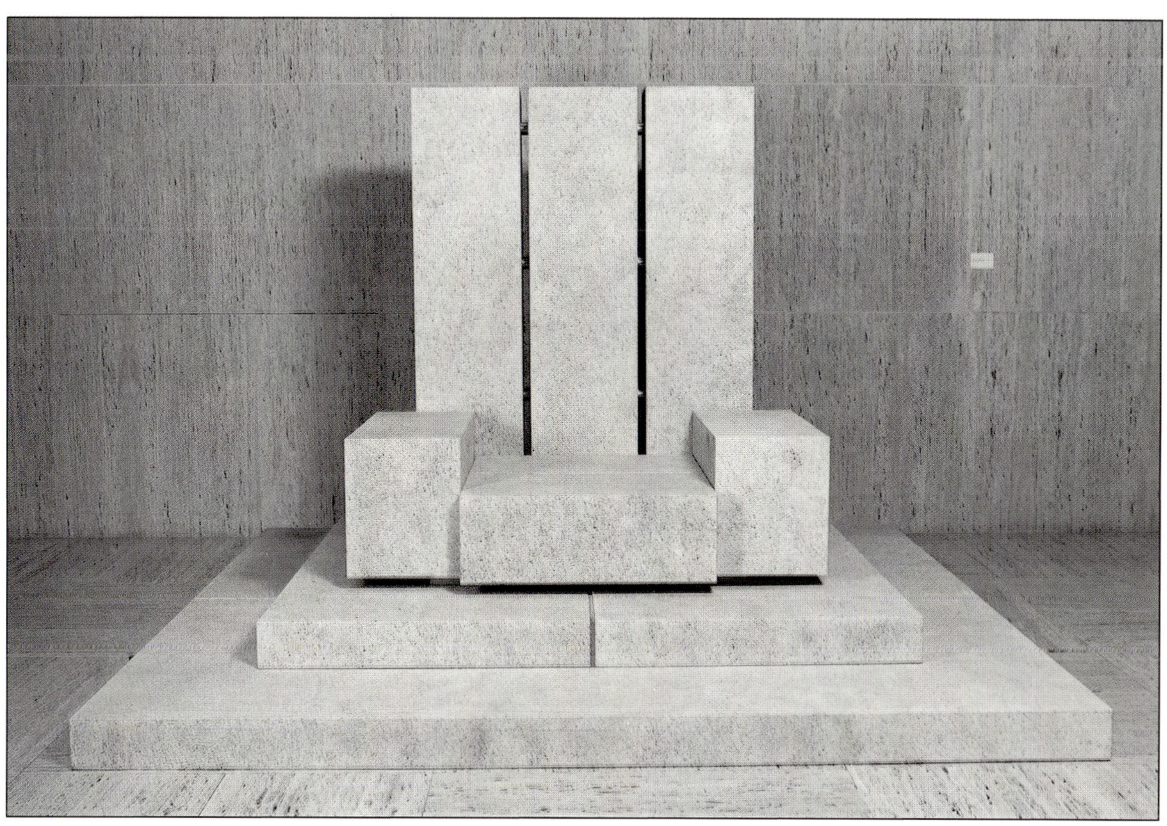

8. *Chair* (model), 1989–90, granite, 6 1/2 × 6 1/2 × 6 1/2 feet, unrealized proposal, collection of the artist

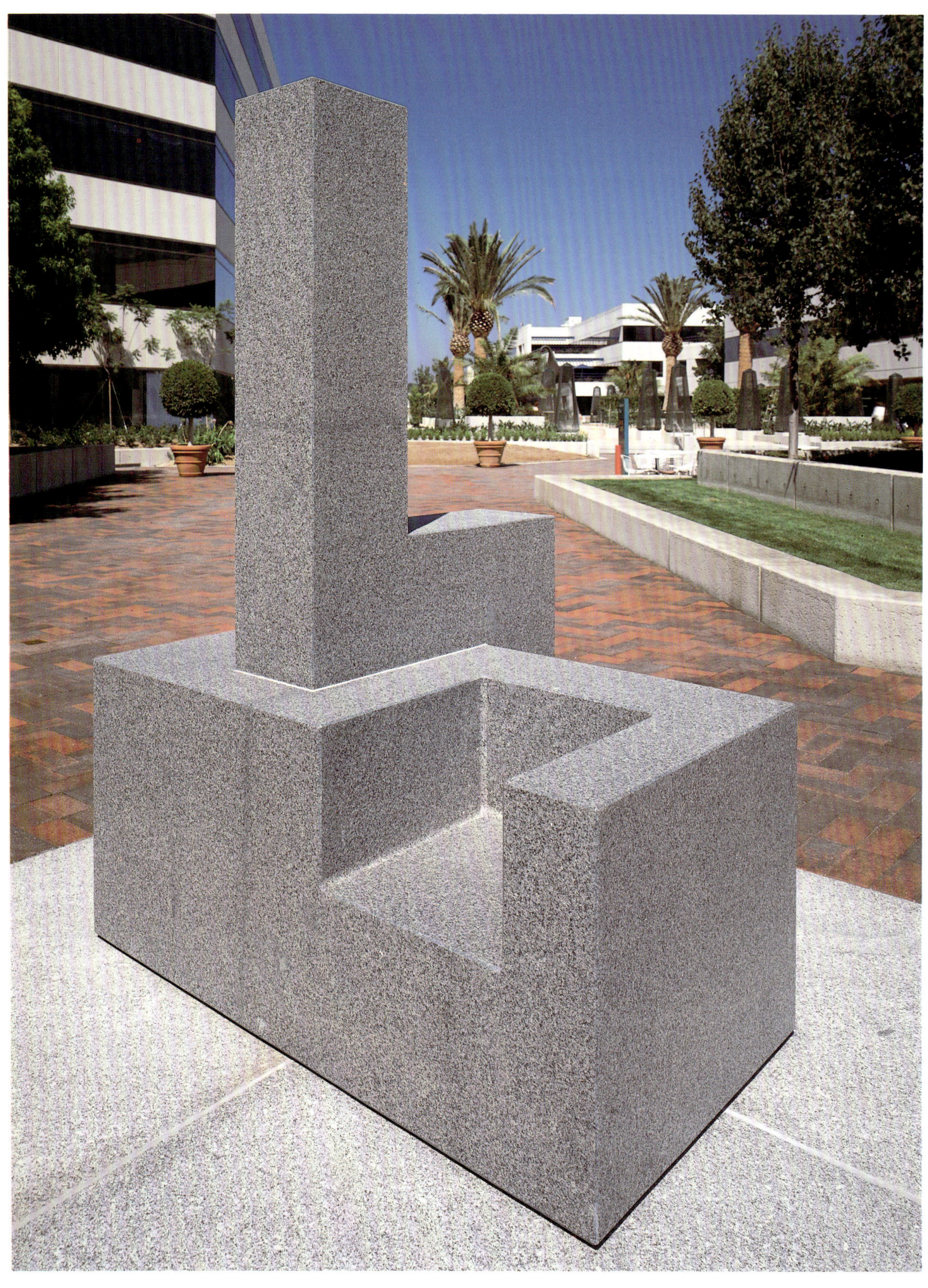

9. *Sitseated,* 1991, granite, 8 × 6 × 4 1/2 feet, Colorado Place,
Santa Monica, California

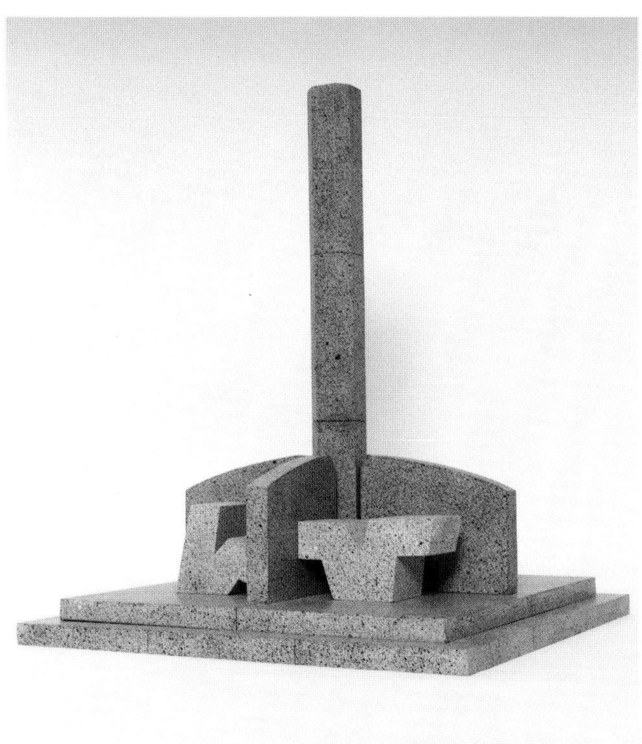

10. Untitled (model), work in progress, granite, 22 × 18 × 18 feet,
outdoor sculpture commission for the McCarren County
Airport, Las Vegas, collection of the artist

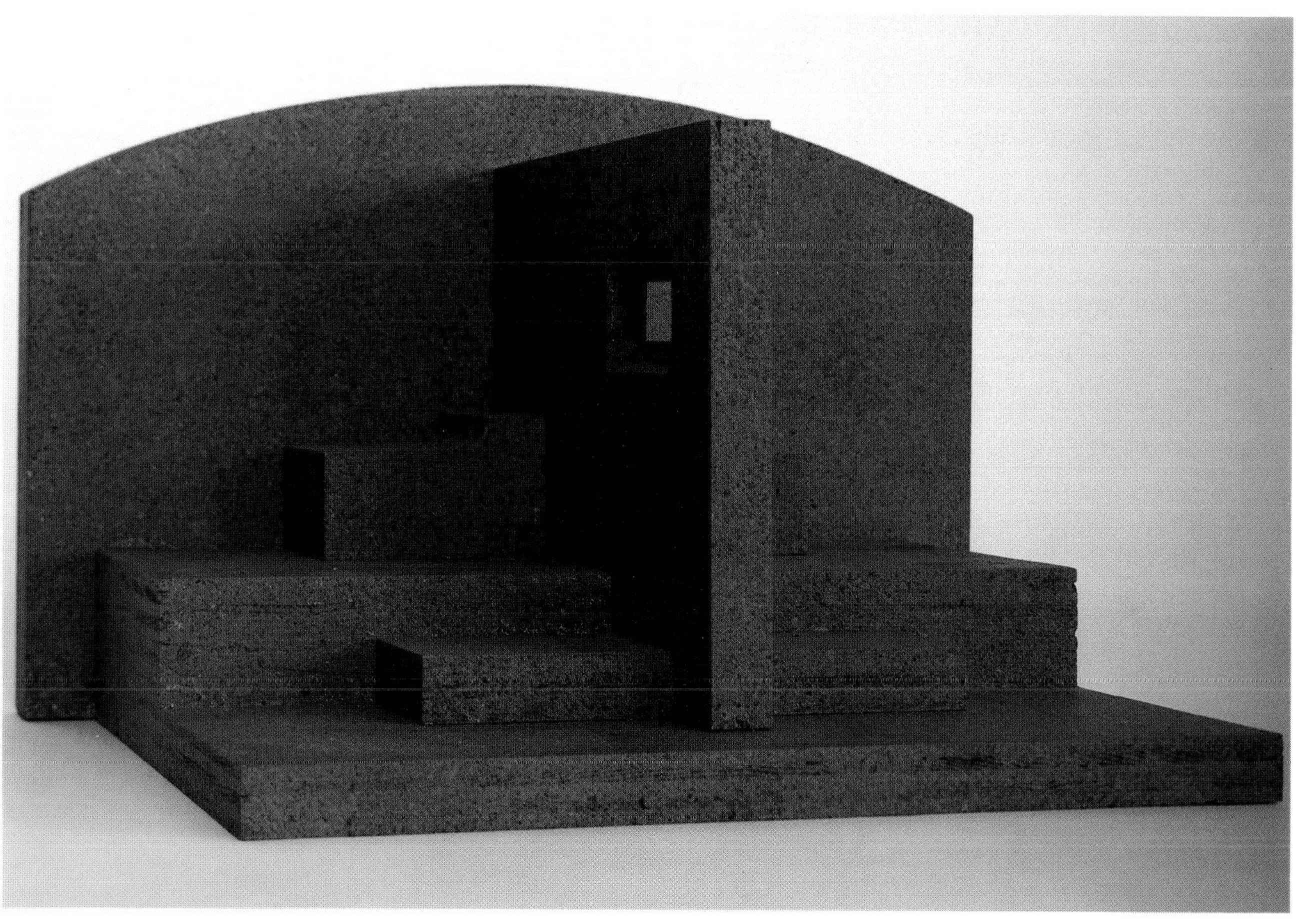

11. Untitled (model), work in progress, granite, 8 1/2 × 7 × 4 2/3 feet, collection of the artist

''Love is expensive,'' says a character in James Baldwin's novel *Another Country.* ''One must put furniture around it or it dies.'' Art is expensive, too: one must put furniture around it or it lives. Frames, *fauteuils,* chandeliers: when these cannot be accumulated in sufficient quantity to suffocate art's driving passions, one must invent a formalist aesthetic to ensure that paintings are indistinguishable from window shades. If that doesn't work, one must consign art to the auctioneer and the magical power of his gavel to turn sculptures into sarcophagi. Failing all else, one must build a museum, the most elaborate piece of furniture yet designed for preventing art's other country from invading our tranquil land.

Or so goes a familiar romantic story: the artist as Sisyphus, doomed by the materiality of his own enterprise never to attain the light place of spiritual freedom, tugged down repeatedly by social gravity into the Valley of Things. It's been some time since you could tell that story with a straight face. When Richard Artschwager began to exhibit art, the heroic struggles of abstract expressionist painting were subsiding amidst the high mirth and dead-pan wit of pop art. I first saw Artschwager's work, a Formica table and chair, in a group show on the pop art movement in 1966. The pop label didn't stick to Artschwager (nor, for that matter, to Johns, Christo, and several others in the show). Still, the grouping enabled these artists to announce with collective force that an impasse had been reached in art's capacity to emancipate either its makers or its beholders from the weight of material life and the embrace of its social conventions. The escape route had become one of those conventions. The narrative of social alienation that had driven art up the hill since the rise of the romantic movement—a pure inside opposed to a corrupt outside—had reached a creative crest.

Worldly success is romantic failure. To establish abstract form as the essence of artistic truth was to institutionalize a lie: the premise that the expression of subjective states of mind could continue indefinitely to release art from its material objecthood. Neither transcendental detachment nor redemptive martyrdom now awaited the artist at the top of his personal hill. That lofty peak was now the prime property of the academy. Its custodians stood ready to welcome the most truculent climber, eager to place his stone upon a pedestal. Even before he started up the hill, the artist's ascent had been converted into history, the most radical form of objectivity we are capable of conferring on human experience. The history of romantic alienation now unfolded as a series of furnished rooms dedicated to the illusion that an artist's

alienation could easily survive such a warm reception. The objects on display might hold the intensity of their moment, but the display itself was proof that the moment had changed. How, as we toured these rooms, could we continue to see artists as the embattled visionaries of another country? How could they continue to regard themselves as outcasts from this one? How could we continue to accept as living an idea that spoke with history's certitude?

Art might no longer issue visas to another country, but it defined a place from which we might look afresh at this one. With *Table and Chair,* Artschwager invited us to pull up a seat, take the load off, rethink the categories to which material objects are assigned. Why are some occupied by bodies, others by *zeitgeists?* What implicit hierarchies are called upon—and denied—in dispatching an object to a gallery or a department store? Initially shocking for breaking the formalist taboo against representation, *Table and Chair* was disturbing for inviting us to recognize that abstract form was representational also: of progress, subjectivity, Freud, above all of art itself, for by mid-century the abstract form applied to canvas was a sign for art, its denotation as firmly nailed down as green for go, black for death, heart for love.

Often, Artschwager's works looked like analogues for the process of aesthetic apprehension. We had illicitly tried to put ourselves in the pictorialized flatness of abstract paintings. Artschwager hung up a mirror. Since we weren't supposed to see ourselves, his mirror offered no reflection. To accompany the academic taming of art's wild ways, Artschwager rolled out a piano—that archetypal symbol of domesticated romanticism—an instrument that played its tune each time we looked at it (no need for guilt over unpracticed scales). Since pictures had been forbidden to turn a window on the outside world, Artschwager showed us that window smudged, through disuse, or prohibition, framing a view as gray as we'd expect any ideologically oppressed world to look.

These works of art had cast off their disguises of art's otherworldliness. Many of them came down from walls and stepped off pedestals to enter into social space, like fashion models at informal, lunchtime showings. Still, they often depended for their effects on the spaces in which we saw them; they relied on our consciousness of the gallery and the otherworldliness implicit in its architecture: its power of metamorphosis, its taboos against touch, its ability to dispense with frames because such spaces are frames already. With the ''blps''—oval shaped, art's primal signature cartouche—Artschwager relaxes his reliance on this space, reducing to minimal, even peripheral means the form required to trigger a viewer's awareness that art is going on. In a recent series of outdoor sculptures, Artschwager has vacated the purified enclosure of art space and entered deeper into the realm of things. He has left the realm of Do Not Touch and entered the world of Walk/Don't Walk, the realm of architecture, utility, and visual disorder, the place where the sky comes in. You can literally as well as figuratively sit down on an Artschwager now. From here, it's easier to see the urban dimension that has figured in Artschwager's art all along.

A sculpture that resembles a chair does not only provoke the idea that works of art may function as pieces of furniture. It also opens up a vista on all that furniture that has aspired to the condition of art: chairs, and also buildings, streetscapes, towns—the whole range of objects that lie on the far side of the line dividing art rom design. Artschwager, legendarily, spent much of his youth on that far side, not only as a craftsman of furniture, but also as a student of Amédée Ozenfant, a framer, with Le Corbusier, of concepts fundamental to modern urbanism. Of course, having elected to work within the context of galleries and museums, Artschwager has chosen to be identified as an artist; he is not an architect or a designer, however provocatively his work may push at the borders around these fields. That is why it's understandable that Artschwager's work is seldom examined in relationship to design.

Yet Artschwager's early craft work is not just a biographical entry, not just a source of visual forms, not just a job he left behind. It is also a point of connection to historical developments in architecture and design. This line of history, never without pertinence to Artschwager's work, is brought into sharper focus by his recent outdoor sculptures. For in stepping out of the sanctuary of art space, these works reconnect Artschwager to the ''far side'' of his earlier years. *Generations,* a recent outdoor project, occupies a transitional zone between the Elvehjem Museum and the streets of Madison. It is an ideal site to examine this connection: to trace the route that leads from arts and crafts to Frank Lloyd Wright and, through Wright, to the modern landscape on which *Generations* arises.

There's an angle from which Artschwager's ascension from craftsman to artist (let's not pretend that we're talking about a simple exchange of equal privileges here) looks like evidence of a collapsed utopian dream. It is the collapse of Nowhere, the Utopia from which William Morris dispatched his famous *News From Nowhere* in 1890. In this work of his last years, Morris outlined the arts and crafts vision of the future—of our present, a century later. Morris sees a world from which art has been, for all practical purposes, eliminated, or, rather, a world in which all art now serves practical purposes. The aesthetic impulses once channeled into the making of unique precious objects—portraits, altarpieces—has been rerouted toward the objects of everyday life.

Art has become the art of living. Chairs, cupboards, textiles, tables: through an infusion of art's transcendent ideal represented, life itself has been elevated. Human relationships are established on a higher, nobler plane. Political systems are reformed, their benefits no longer flowing toward the few at the expense of the many. Hopes deferred until the entrance into the kingdom of heaven after death are to be gratified on this earth: in the building of roads and houses, the harvesting of crops, the harmonious integration of nature and civilization. Above all, they are gratified at home, in the arrangements of domesticity, the furnishing of private life.

It is this emphasis on the space of privacy that Frank Lloyd Wright makes the basis of his life's work. Though Wright built a handful of spectacular public buildings, and designed many others that were not built, these remained secondary to the residential architecture with which he established the private home as the dominant building type of modern times. Unlike Morris, Wright did not think it was necessary to engage in political action to bring about a better society. He assumed, rather, that Americans had already set in place a political structure conducive to the individual freedom such a society required. Wright's job was to visualize that structure in symbolic, architectural form. Thus, in 1935, nearly half a century after Morris published his literary narrative of Nowhere, Wright unveiled his model and drawings for Broadacre City, his vision of a decentralized urban America.

Described by Wright as the city that is ''everywhere and nowhere,'' Broadacre City is the land of the sovereign individual, the home of the masses freed from urban bondage into the natural paradise of self-realization. Public space in Broadacre City has been virtually reduced to two forms: Nature and the Highway—a setting for ''the natural house'' and the circulation routes required to reach it. It is as though the entire continent of North America has taken on the pattern of one of Morris's floral fabrics. The central city has been eliminated, with possibly some parts preserved in aspic. ''We go occasionally to the graveyards of our ancestors,'' Wright commented in his book *The Disappearing City,* ''so why not to the remains of their cities?''

In many respects, Wright accurately forecast the suburban sprawl of the post-war years. Architecture has been so thoroughly domesticated that we can scarcely imagine a time when small houses played little part in architectural affairs. We now call the poor ''homeless,'' in part because they live in such conspicuous contrast to the population's retreat into the private realm architects have helped to fashion. Public funds maintain highways, while urban streets are left, like landscapes, to God and the weather. We still have cities, of course, but those that have not become graveyards are well on their way to becoming theme parks managed by private operators.

In more fundamental ways, however, decentralization has turned out quite differently from Wright's hopes. Physical decentralization in space has not visibly engendered individual autonomy. On the contrary, it has been accompanied by an intense consolidation of corporate power and a radical homogenization of cultural life. The withdrawal into privacy has produced the paradoxical effect of turning the home into a fragment of public space. Architecture is a social art, and to make the private home into architecture is inevitably to declare that society has a stake there. Wright was well aware that when he was designing a private house, the ''client'' was not the individual who would reside there. The client was the ''American way of life,'' as Wright interpreted it. With its room deodorizers, laundry whiteners, ceremonial living rooms, market-researched decorations, suburban life embodies a normativity as extreme as that of a neoclassic public square.

The domestication of architecture, in other words, has led to a condition remarkably similar to the impasse reached by the oppositional conception of art. The desire for subjective expression has produced conventions of spatial form and social behavior which significantly contradict the myth of individual autonomy that desire sought to make manifest.

Enter Public Art—an entrance prompted, in part, by architecture's retreat into the private realm. The term ''public art'' is something of an oxymoron: even with a social art like architecture we shrink from the idea that art should be a crowd-pleaser. At the same time, the term is redundant: even at the farthest degree of romantic subjectivity, art draws much of its significance from the public discourse the very idea of art provokes. Still, the term is useful in signaling that artists do have a contract with society and that the terms of that contract are in a constant state of renegotiation. Artschwager prefers the term ''outdoor sculpture,'' no wonder. Why call some of his work ''public art'' when all of it, indoors or out, reflects both the prospect of public reception and a grasp of art's roots in public ceremony? The fact is, there would scarcely be a ''public art'' today, or a critical approach to work by such artists as Scott Burton, Siah Armajani and Ned Smythe, if Artschwager hadn't set out his tables and chairs thirty years ago.

For Frank Lloyd Wright, ''architecture'' was the organic consequence of ideas he worked out primarily in the design of interior space. For Artschwager, similarly, outdoor sculpture is a logical extension of ideas his art has long embodied. Yet with the penetration of architectural enclosure, Artschwager shifts from an engagement with design as a point of reference to an engagement with architecture. He surrenders the protection of gallery space, with its built-in framework of metaphysical speculation, and enters a realm where people are looking for a place to sit down and enjoy a hot dog. In this realm, an artist not only alters our perception of the world but materially alters the world we perceive.

Sitting/Stance, the first of Artschwager's large outdoor pieces to be realized, was commissioned in 1984 for Battery Park City, a new office and residential complex built on ninety-two acres of landfill at the southern tip of Manhattan. The New York state officials who organized this project adopted a strategic use of architecture for economic objectives. Their goal was to persuade middle class New Yorkers to remain in the city instead of leaving for the suburbs. Toward that end, the master plan's design guidelines, conceived in 1979, were modeled after buildings in older New York neighborhoods of stabilized affluence, such as West End Avenue, Gramercy Park, and Gracie Square. Masonry bases, brick facades, and articulated building tops were among the features architects were required to incorporate in their designs. While apartments in Battery Park City are as cramped as most new ''luxury'' housing, the exteriors recall the stolid dignity of prized ''pre-war'' buildings.

Battery Park City is an eerie place. The attempt to connect new development to New York's architectural traditions had instead generated a powerful sense of dislocation, for we are separated from prewar architecture not only by a war, but by the historical gulf of the modern movement and its rejection of traditional forms. Battery Park City was, in fact, designed in express opposition to modern architectural forms and, especially, modern concepts of urbanism. Earlier proposals for the site had called for vast concrete megastructures, or the ''towers in a park'' formula conceived by Le Corbusier. The 1979 master plan called for a return to the forms of traditional streets, with sidewalks, storefronts, and stoops. In addition, the grid system of lower Manhattan streets was extended onto the new site, though a six-lane highway at the site's western edge ruled out the likelihood of through traffic.

The absence of traffic in fact accounts for much of the eeriness of Battery Park City. The traditional design of the streets accentuates that absence, for the streets evoke in appearance a public realm that does not truly exist here. Cars, we begin to sense, define the public realm in cities. They are signs of democratic access. Without them, we feel we're trespassing on private property; as indeed we are, for despite the design controls imposed by the state, this place is the creation of private development. Even Battery Park City's ambitious program of public art heightens the impression of a privileged enclave. The sculptures are a luxury touch, like concierge service and designer kitchens. This place is a theme park version of New York, a city where art has long been a major theme.

In a preliminary version, Artschwager's project for Battery Park City was literally connected to the architecture by a slim metal column that rose from the ground and attached itself to the side of a nearby apartment building. Even without that physical link, the realized version of *Sitting/Stance* draws on the architectural context and the thinking that shaped it. The design guidelines sought to create by executive control the kind of environment that once developed without it, and it has that look of the artificially natural, the planned spontaneous, the authoritarian casual. In *Sitting/Stance,* two oversized chairs face each other in a dialogue of the rigid and the relaxed: a ramrod-stiff, Egyptoid throne (fig. 1) squares off against a laid-back lounge chair (fig. 2). The work as a whole projects an oddly suburban mood, a summertime air of odds and ends thrown together for seating at a backyard barbecue. The impression of patio living may seem at odds with the architects' efforts to evoke a crisp, sophisticated urbanity. Yet that note turns out to be the right one, for despite its urbane yearnings, Battery Park City has the sleepy, detached soul of a Westchester bedroom town. Its streets simulate New York streets the way a suburban subdivision's curving roads simulate country lanes.

The most explicitly historical elements at Battery Park City are the cast iron lamp posts that illuminate the streets and also line the site's riverfront esplanade to the west of *Sitting/Stance.* Symbols of pre-war New York, the lamps are a kind of fetish and are treated as such by Artschwager, who enclosed one of the lamps within the protective embrace of a metal armature, enshrining the lamp as a display. The form playfully makes visible the aura of preciousness which Battery Park City's architects exploit but do not acknowledge: if cities are to become museums, then they must have vitrines.

Art is too young to die. At least, Morris's hopes for art's disappearance have been deferred for now. Far from subsiding gracefully into the form of plates, chairs, and carpets, art has risen irresistibly up the ladder of cultural prestige. There it sits, embodied in the form of the museum and in the idea we often hear that museums have inherited from churches the task of providing an accessible repository for civilization's highest values. The equation of art with religion is deforming to both, even offensive considering how convincingly in recent years artists have impersonated tycoons. Yet even those like myself who doubt that art can adequately serve a religious function must grant that art has gone far toward occupying the place formerly claimed by religion in the ancient dualism between matter and spirit. Without even

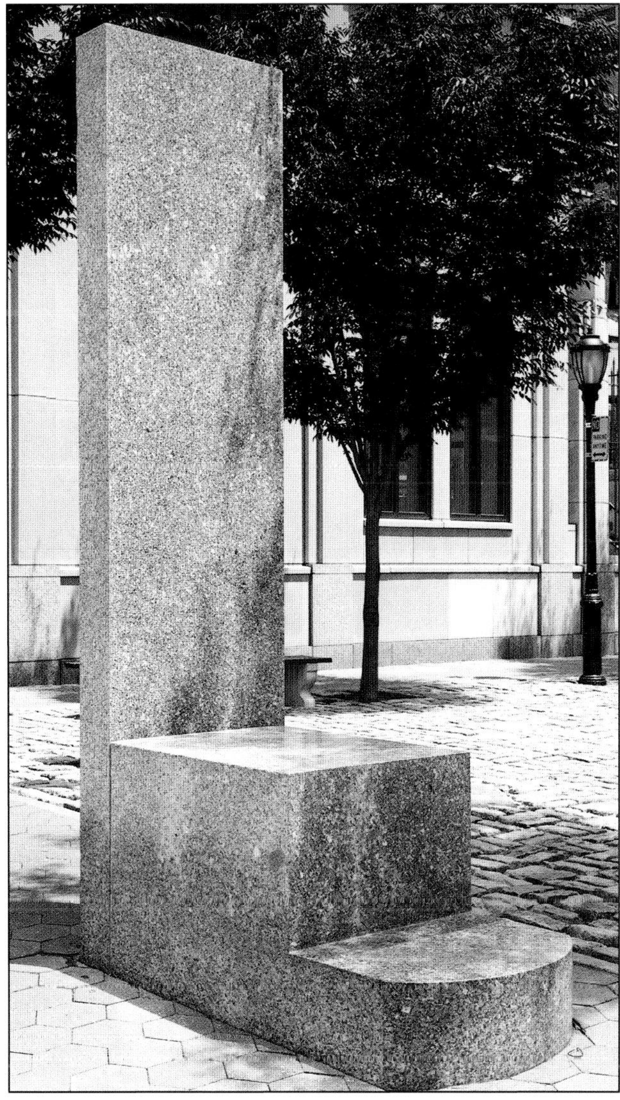

Fig. 1. *Sitting/Stance,* 1984–88, Battery Park City, New York

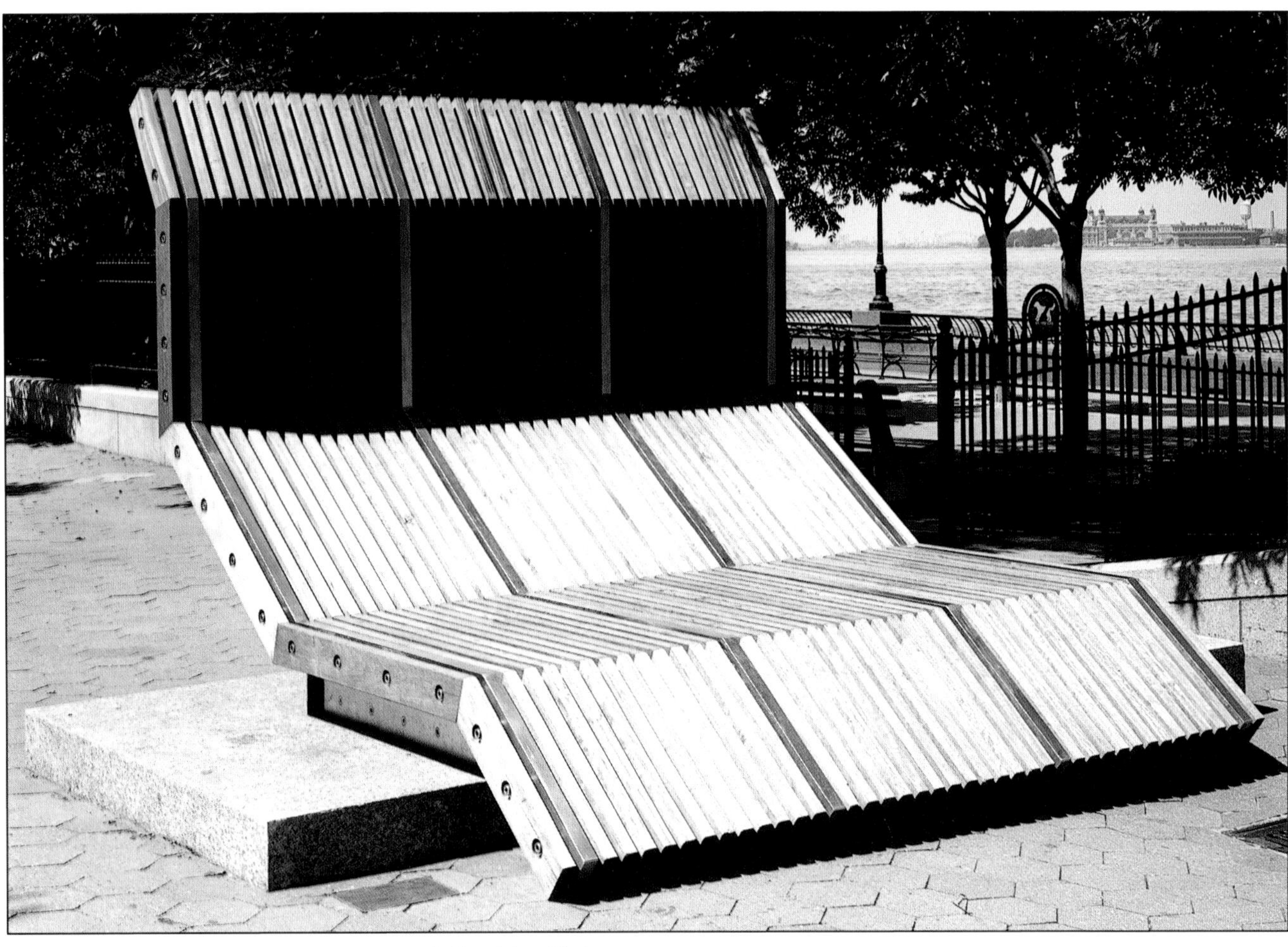

Fig. 2. *Sitting/Stance,* 1984–88, Battery Park City, New York

having to think about it, we embrace material standards (economic growth, scientific objectivity) as universal measures of reality. With some optimism, and with art's roots in religious ceremony for justification, we've elected art to stand in for the universal spirit our fragmented religious life has failed to provide.

The modern version of the old dualism has taken more than one form. For Kandinsky, abstract painting staked art to a stance of opposition, to a fight against what he termed ''the nightmare of materialism.'' For Morris, on the other hand, art's ideal relationship to matter was not opposition but fusion. The explicit medievalism of Morris's designs evoked an idealized view of the middle ages in which social harmony is fostered by unifying faith in a transcendent order. Yet even Morris's desire for fusion did not collapse the dualism entirely. ''Nowhere,'' after all, was a projection of the distance Morris insinuated between himself and the materialism of the industrial age.

As a citizen in a country that has never known a unifying religious practice, Frank Lloyd Wright endured even greater pressure than Morris from the materialism of his day. Son of a Unitarian preacher, Wright was brought up in a nursery decorated with

prints of the great European cathedrals placed there by his mother in hopes that Wright would grow up to be the architect he in fact became. In later life, Wright would boast of taking as much care with the design of small houses as architects once spent on cathedrals. In his attempt to gain spiritual ground without caving in to European tradition, Wright modeled several dwellings after Mayan temples. Norris Kelly Smith observed that in his domestic designs Wright consistently treated dining ''as if it were liturgical in nature,'' which for Wright, of course, it was. It was communion for believers in the power of organic architecture to raise civilization to a higher plane.

Wright's Guggenheim Museum made a home for spiritualist abstraction like Kandinsky's in the capital of matter, New York City. The Guggenheim's spiral form originated in a project designed for cars: Wright's unbuilt Gordon Strong Automobile Objective, designed in 1925. Later, he employed it for a Pittsburgh parking garage. Archetypal symbol of American materialism, the car was for Wright the ultimate embodiment of his philosophy of individual freedom. By the 1930s, in fact, he had transformed arts and crafts into a movement of arts and cars. To Wright we owe the car port and the transformation of the American house into a glorified garage.

I have no idea whether Richard Artschwager recognizes any form of transcendent entity that the word ''spirit'' typically denotes. Yet his earliest work established as a recurring theme the interdependence of the physical and the metaphysical. His 1963 *Chair* is the primal chair, the Egyptian throne from which all chairs descend. Symbol of highest authority in the theocracy from which, by tradition, Western art arose, the chair is executed in materials associated with mass production. Its prie-dieu form suggests that the book in *Book III (Laocoön)* (1981) is The Book, the word of God which, with Gutenberg, becomes the basis for all mechanical production. The stiff formality of *Three Dinners* (1984–85) recalls Wright's liturgical repasts, while Artschwager's explicit reference to Wright in his 1974 *Johnson Wax Building* depicts an office interior Wright fashioned after an Egyptian hypostyle hall in the hope of conferring spiritual dignity on the American workplace.

The objects neither evaporate into metaphysical thin air nor do they dissolve themselves into matter. They embody the dualism within themselves, proclaiming a dual citizenship in the physical and metaphysical worlds. They propose that spirit and matter, while not the same thing, are yet two aspects of a single entity, the heads and tails of our Western cultural currency. The proposition coincides with the Eastern perception that the two sides are joined.

In a space between art and cars, Artschwager's *Generations* sets up a hinge between a building type and a contemporary city. The Elvehjem Museum is an architectural hybrid. The building's vocabulary is recognizably modern, yet its plate glass windows reveal a grand staircase rising within. This traditional feature, symbol of a master's ascent to the pantheon, was typically eliminated from modern museums, such as the Museum of Modern Art in New York, which sought to reinforce a sense of spatial and cultural continuity between the museum and urban life. In Madison, the combination of Beaux Arts and Bauhaus turned out to be less than inviting. This deficiency has provided the happy occasion for Artschwager's commission.

Generations begins with a functional program: to declare the building's identity and to entice the public to enter. Founded as a teaching facility, the Elvehjem seeks to enhance its identity as a community resource. Like a Gothic cathedral's sculpted tympanum, *Generations* beckons the eye, prepares the mind, and lures the body inside. This centripetal program serves a centrifugal purpose: to lure people inside is to encourage a dispersal of art's immaterial values through visitors as they exit.

The work picks up its vocabulary from the museum's ornamental lighting fixtures and its decorative screen of trees: forlorn architectural accessories designed to soften the harshness of the building's exterior. Physically enlarged, visually isolated, these elements are amplified from the scale of the standardized and meaningless to that of the unique and significant. Like Napoleon, Columbus, or Civic Virtue, the tree and the lamp perch atop columns, as if to rebuke their dumb architectural ancestors for not making more of themselves. Think of what a tree, a spherical lamp, might be: Apollonian light! Promethean fire! The sphere's embodiment of perfection! The tree as parent of the first column! As symbol of culture's growth out of nature! The museum as a place of light! Or think of Wright and the geometric abstraction of architectural form which was his great gift to Europe's nascent modern movement. But the dumb ancestors are part of the message. Together with Artschwager's amplified versions, they lead us toward the museum as a place where ideas are enlarged to their fullest potential.

The work is a triptych on hierarchy: tree and light appear before us in Hi, Medium, and Lo. If we read the three ''panels'' frontally from right to left, as we read a book, they invert the traditional hierarchy of the museum program. Instead of ascending to the pantheon, the tree descends to street level, progressing from a height so platonic that no natural tree can live there, to the earthly plane where we can gather in its shade. The light descends from a height so lofty we may despair of attaining its perfection to a plane beneath our feet, where its rays dissolve in a pool of water: the universal solvent, the gift to the traveler, the offering, in Eastern tradition, to life itself.

The museum stands on high cultural ground. It is already a place of light, even if natural light must be reduced to protect the objects that are presented within as evidence of human enlightenment. Artschwager's highest tree is an artificial tree, each needle painstakingly produced and fitted; like the images inside, this machine-made evergreen requires climate control for its conservation, the mechanical gauges visible on the column's metal shaft. Reversing the Vitruvian custom that columns evolved out of trees, the column also essays hierarchy; columns cannot stand, much less reach skyward, unless they are planted on firm ground.

In a recent conversation, Artschwager indicated that his is not the kind of art for which any old interpretation will do. Some, evidently, would fit better than others. This reading of *Generations* is, however, my own—I haven't asked the artist what specific significance trees, lamps, columns, and pools of water hold for him—and it would not surprise me if what I see doesn't square with what he set out to make, or takes in only part of it. Speculation is the risk an artist takes when he ventures into a public space, or into those mental recesses he chooses to make visible. There is no need to make public and durable a work that could disclose its meanings on brief inspection by one observer. And a measure of ambiguity is a good thing to set in front of an art museum, for when the public enters here we face the risk of accepting too narrow an interpretation of the objects we behold.

We come here, in part, to learn meanings. Indeed, if there is any merit to the idea that art has inherited the place of religion, the parallel lies not only in vague allusions to spiritual life but in the concrete, not to say mundane, toils of scholarship required to construct proper meanings for visual forms. Semantic stability was once a function of cathedrals. Rose windows, statues of the saints, illuminated manuscripts: these images were not only visual narratives for the illiterate but also emblems of church authority to declare all art a language of faith. Museums display their authority with words: wall plaques, recorded tours, catalogues, essays such as this one, texts that weave together strands of history, philosophy, and biography to show that in this or that context a circle or a sphere stands for the perfection of a supreme being; an integrated self; the restlessness of desire; the void; even the literary notion that art's purpose is not to mean but be.

A museum is not a library. Words are second-class citizens here. A visitor who leans forward to read a text on the wall may momentarily fear exposure as a visual illiterate. In theory, we owe to formalism art's freedom from the function of literary illustration, subordinate to ideas outside its own language. Catholic with a small c, formalism overarches differences in content; all objects are manifested in forms. But who, peering up at the ceiling of the Sistine Chapel, could take what they see as illustration, in any way subordinate to religious doctrine? On the contrary, we are more likely to see religion as the scaffold that enabled Michelangelo to reach the place where he could exercise his own authority to

the fullest extent. And in the presence of that exercise the question of meaning slips away. We don't need a lexicon on the sibyls and their attributes to recognize creation. We can see for ourselves that Michelangelo is confined by no text, that his conception of a ceiling exceeds its functional description as the underside of a surface that keeps out rain. Looking up, we leave the place of meaning and enter the place of meaningfulness. That place calls for no mediation of priests and curators, though they can help us with a scaffold to get up there. An artist has hollowed out this place; it is up to us to furnish it.

I was impressed to learn that in his carpenter years Artschwager once made altars for use aboard ships. It seems to me that he has gone on making them, though for thirty years now the voyage has been his own. Singular in its course, it has passed within hailing distance of many ports where art has done substantial trading (the movements with which we like to label art, from pop to public and others in between), each with a distinctive topography, local customs, exotic wares, even a native tongue, or, as we say, critical vocabulary. Generous, independent, Artschwager's passage is an exemplary one to keep in mind as we approach a building to look at art. What we see here is also a language of faith: not in a god or even a *zeitgeist* but in the premise that to witness any exercise of internal authority is a profound stimulant to one's own. Museums are not only places of learning; they are places to abandon the world of learning and enter the world of realization where art objects are formed. At a certain point, or repeatedly, the balance of power must shift, the hierarchy reverse itself and point away from the artist's to the beholder's act of realization. Someone had the idea to place a tree atop a column and set a bubble of light beside it. They may not mean the tree the human race climbed down from or the radiance to which civilization aspires; perhaps they say nothing about the need for art to serve the living as a condition for giving artists the license to soar. Yet such possibilities come flying forth from a beholder as naturally as iron particles drawn toward a magnet. Then they are in the world, along with objects, to be beheld.

Herbert Muschamp
Parsons School of Design